44 0097...

D1424584

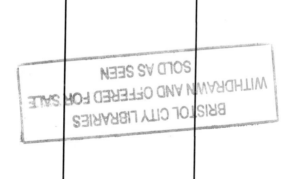

HOW TO BE A BUDDHIST MILLIONAIRE

9 practical steps to being happy
in a materialist world

MATT JARDINE

Published in 2020 by Short Books Ltd
Unit 316, ScreenWorks, 22 Highbury Grove,
London, N5 2ER

10 9 8 7 6 5 4 3 2 1

A CIP catalogue record for this book is available
from the British Library.

ISBN: 978-1-78072-424-9

Cover design by Evie Dunne

Printed at CPI Group (UK) Ltd, Croydon, CR0 4YY

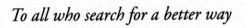

To all who search for a better way

Contents

Introduction

'Even the Dalai Lama's robes cost money.
Although His Holiness may not have to reach
into his own wallet, someone somewhere will
have to pick up the tab.'

— Anonymous

For your own sake, answer honestly. If you had a
million pounds would you be living your current
life? Would you be doing the work you currently do?
If the answer is yes, and you are happy with that, then
congratulations. If the answer is no and you are not happy,
don't worry, you are not alone and this book is for you.

Polls reveal that many are not living their ideal life
in regard to work and career. Indeed, it appears that as
many as seven out of ten of us in the western world are
not leaping out of bed to embrace the work day ahead.
Try asking the million-pound question above at the next

social gathering you attend and test these numbers for yourself. You'll be surprised.

If you are not living the life of your dreams, then what are you doing? Probably working too hard for too little, right?

With a third of our lives spent working and another third sleeping, little time is left in which to do the things that inspire, lift our souls and fully engage us mentally, physically, emotionally and spiritually. This seems an awful waste of life to me.

But there is hope. If the polls are correct, nearly a third, 30%, *are* living fulfilling lives and doing work that they adore – work that they would do irrespective of the money.

By doing purposeful, profitable work these '30-percenters' are doubling the amount of time spent doing things that, to them, have great meaning.

Not only are they doing work for which they happily get out of bed in the morning, rather than crawl back under the covers after hitting the snooze button, they are meeting financial obligations while doing so.

This book is going to show you how you can too.

To be considered a success, modern life and the economy demand constant growth. In our financially driven world if we are not growing, we are regarded as failing. With the pressures caused by this economic model, we must sprint just to stand still. We end up chained to money and making life choices that are mostly driven by economics and the demands of our bosses, customers and financial obligations.

With money so central to our universe, it is undeniable that it has become our master, our God even, whether we care to admit it or not.

We might insist and may genuinely believe that we are the 'captains of our fate and the masters of our soul' but it is the very often the things in life that we spend unconsciously denying, avoiding or appeasing that are at the helm, not us. Money has a deep-rooted hold over us all.

However, this is not a book about making money or a bible of economics. There are plenty of other books to teach you about wealth creation. From these you may learn how to look after the pennies that have fallen down the back of the couch. You may work out how to sell your tenth apartment for impressive profits. You may also learn about downsizing and retirement strategies and use the savings to buy a one-bedroom canal boat to sail off into the sunset of your old age.

This is not one of those books because, whatever the financial approach you employ, all money strategies are inherently flawed. By trying to escape poverty and amass wealth, and however successful you are at this, you are still bound by the rules and laws of money.

We are all familiar with the mantra handed down to us from our parents and our society: go to school, study hard, graduate from university, get a good job, settle down, save, invest, support a family, retire well and die, taking none of our money with us!

It is a game the majority of us are taught to play. Some will win, while others will lose. When was the last time you sat down and questioned the healthiness of this default mode of living? Is it time to investigate alternative options?

This book is concerned with finding another way, a new game with different rules. It will try to play a game where to win, in the modern sense of the word, doesn't necessarily mean to succeed, and where, even in a state of 'loss', you will still look forward to the new day.

When looking up at the heavens on a clear bright night and marvelling at the stars, the planets and the universe, our minds are not usually filled with musings on money:

'Wow, I wonder who pays for all those stars?'

'Has anyone considered franchising the planets?'

'Who are the majority shareholders of the universe?'

And yet, while we theoretically understand that finances do not sit at the centre of the outer cosmos, we cannot escape the fact that they do, more often than not, sit at the centre of ours.

Instinctively, we suspect that there is more to life than work, bills and deadlines. Humans have questioned life's meaning since the dawn of time. Indeed the institutions of religion, philosophy and science evolved, for better or worse, from an attempt to make sense of the world and reveal life's higher purpose. Even the most pessimistic atheists among us, those who believe we live a mechanical and spiritless life until we die, have, at one time or another, also looked up at the stars and considered their source. After all, even a mechanical universe must have an origin.

Scientists, philosophers and religious leaders have more in common than they care to admit; namely, the fathoming of life. But it is religion that has taken the brunt of criticism in recent times.

The stature of organised religion has changed over the centuries. As a consequence of religion's inherent frailties and its scrutiny under the microscope of science, many people are embracing a more 'spiritual', rather than religious, set of beliefs. As critical thinkers we are cutting out the middleman to the divine and forming our own unique opinions on the meaning of life.

We are not, however, throwing the baby out with the holy water by turning to alternative religions and self-appointed searches for existential knowledge. Our religious forerunners have done much to pave the way for where we are today. We are merely upgrading and trusting, at long last, in our own voice to describe 'God' – just as the Taoists once chose their yin-yang symbology, and the Nichiren Buddhists their Lotus Sutra chant, to explain God. We are free to explain the unexplainable source of all things in any way we choose.

Do not fear! Just as this is not a book about how to get rich quick, neither is it a new-age or religious book. This is not a book that will require you to stand in front of a mirror to chant, affirm or visualise.

What it will do, though, is ask you to open your mind to ideas and teachings that may be unfamiliar. As uncommon as these ideas might be to your current way of thinking, it is precisely their being different that make them valuable to you. After all, if your way of living were working, you wouldn't be reading this book. All of these ideas, no matter how unusual, have been tried and tested in the field of modern life by myself and the other 30-percenters, I can assure you.

So our task here is to unite the two extremes that are neatly symbolised by the ancient Chinese symbol of yin-yang. At one extreme is the lighter side of yin, characterised by wisdom, imagination, peacefulness, relaxation, satisfaction, persistence and introversion. This is the image of the 'starving artist', who is creatively fulfilled and in touch with their life's true meaning but severely lacking in the material world where they must ply their trade. They may be happy but they are broke.

At the other extreme is the darker side of yang, characterised by action, ambition, bravery, extroversion, excitement, adventurousness and bravado. The image of the 'ruthless banker' reigns supreme. This focused 'killer' of the business arena has mastered the material world and amassed wealth and financial success of which the starving artist could only dream, but at what cost? Kindness, compassion, health, family time and a life of meaning and deep fulfilment?

Can these two extremes be united by a middle way?

Must one be sacrificed to embrace the other? Is it possible to break free of financial shackles and search for a life of higher purpose? Can we live our true callings and deepest passions and still be successful in a modern materialist world? To answer these questions we will need to enlist some help.

There is one old-school religion, positioned at the crossroads of science, philosophy and modern spirituality that is still as relevant today as it was 2,000 years ago in the far-eastern lands where it emerged: Buddhism.

Buddhism and some of its principles feature in much of this book – although it is not a book about Buddhism. I do not claim to have an academically profound understanding of this ancient system, but I can offer hard-earned lessons and experiences as a lay Buddhist for more than 25 years.

The turning point for me occurred over ten years ago. I was standing in the grounds of Ryozenji, a Buddhist temple on the Japanese island of Shikoku, watching the orange and white flashes on the scales of koi carp swimming in a pond.

Ryozenji is the start and end point of the 88 Temple Pilgrimage (called the Hachi-ju-Hachi by the Japanese). This is Japan's iconic holy trail, much like the Camino de Santiago de Compostela in Spain. I had just completed 1,400km in 30 days on foot, and had visited all 88 Buddhist temples necessary for the pilgrimage to be considered accomplished.

This life-changing experience ultimately became the subject of my first book, *The Hardest Path*. A circuitous pilgrimage such as the 88 mimics, in microcosm, all of the possible experiences, emotions, thoughts and subsequent actions that a human may have in the macrocosm of a lifetime.

The benefit of seeing all your thoughts and emotions exposed as you walk hundreds of miles is that you can no longer avoid who you are, what you are thinking and how you react to everyday experiences. There is no distraction either to hide your frailties or deny your strengths. While on pilgrimage, you live your life in technicolour, not because you have entered some strange spiritual domain, but because with nothing to do other than walking, resting and eating, there are no obscurations. Your mind, body and soul are in the spotlight and at last you are observing how they behave. After all, what else is there to do on a 1,400km walk around an island?

In such open terrain, geographically, physically, mentally and emotionally, lessons are learned. While these may vary from one pilgrim to another, depending on what each of us needs to learn, some degree of personal insight will occur. I learned nine lessons and these form the backbone of this book. As I stood looking into Ryozenji's fishpond, after being irrevocably changed by the journey, it occurred to me that what I had learned on the 88 Temple Pilgrimage would mean nothing unless I could take it home. If those nine lessons could not be brought back, translated into an accessible language, used amid all the noise and chaos of daily life and shared with others, then they were of no use.

My desire to bring these lessons back home was partly altruistic and partly selfish. I did indeed want to share the life-changing lessons for the benefit of others, as holy men had told me to do, but I also wanted to assuage a nagging doubt.

Would these great insights hold true once I had left the sanctity of the holy trail? The Buddhists call it 'coming down from the mountain'. What good is insight, spiritual or otherwise, if it cannot help you and others while leading an ordinary life?

I have spoken of the games and rules we won't be playing by: the tactics of cut-throat economies and the incomplete doctrines of religion, philosophy or science. Nor will we, in some hasty search for a 'spiritual' backdrop to our lives, be handing ourselves over to uncorroborated new-age fads.

Instead, I propose that we play a game pitched on the field of life, allowing us to learn directly from our experiences, mistakes and triumphs. We will seek to find the path between prosperity and purpose – and discover that the two things are not necessarily antithetical.

I have come to refer to those who manage to walk the tightrope between meaning and money as 'Buddhist Millionaires'. But let me be clear: it is not necessary to be either a Buddhist to live a meaningful and purpose-driven life, or a millionaire to indicate that you are a success in business or the workplace. Whatever term you choose to describe yourself after discovering that it is indeed possible to live a fulfilling life within a material world often at odds with higher purpose is up to you.

It will be a fun game certainly, and I will never ask you to believe in something that cannot be proved or demonstrated. This is a book of doing, not one of believing or following unquestioningly.

Part I of the book will look at the default beliefs about money that shape our world and lives. We will consider the pain and difficulty that a 'money first' attitude causes us and take advice from teammates, coaches and advisors that we will meet along the way.

By facing our mental paradigms head on, we can begin to question their validity and investigate whether perhaps our assumptions about money and work are not entirely correct. If there is more to life than money, what is it?

In Part II, we will investigate the necessity for human beings to live meaningful lives, rather than exist solely for the pursuit and accumulation of wealth.

We will look at the limitations of traditional ideas about what imbues a life with meaning and, instead, offer exercises to uncover your personal and unique life's calling, giving you the confidence not only to define it, but to covet it.

In Part III, the heart of the book, we will put you on the path of the Buddhist Millionaire. We will show you how to live a life of meaning and make it into a successful, financially rewarding career, by following nine key lessons.

Part III will feature true stories and advice from people who are successfully walking the path of the Buddhist Millionaire, from award-winning chefs, athletes and artists to bankers and charity workers.

My ultimate hope for this book is that it motivates, inspires and guides you to a life where you are living your passion and making it pay. I want to help you create a new life, where in future, when someone asks you, 'If you had a million pounds, would you be living your current life?' your answer might just be, 'Hell, yeah.'

Part I

The Path of Money

The 'Everywhere Nowhere'

'The most difficult subjects can be explained to the most slow-witted man if he has not formed any idea of them already; but the simplest thing cannot be made clear to the most intelligent man if he is firmly persuaded that he knows already, without a shadow of doubt, what is laid before him.'

– Leo Tolstoy

'Empty your cup so that it may be filled.'

– Bruce Lee

Albert Einstein, Mark Twain, Benjamin Franklin and Alcoholics Anonymous have all been attributed with the saying: 'The definition of insanity is doing the same thing over and over and expecting a different result.' While technically untrue – the definition of insanity is not this and probably wasn't written by any of the above – the saying nevertheless makes a good point. If we are constantly struggling, unhappy and making the same mistakes, then we need to change course and find a better way.

We are all creatures of habit, landlocked into our lives by unchallenged beliefs, daily habits and self-perpetuating choices that strengthen the cycle. Although repetition and practice can indeed lead competence and even mastery of a given task, without care this mastery can work against us.

There is an old Cherokee legend known as 'The Two Wolves', that recounts a conversation between an elder tribesman and a young boy. Much like the polar extremes depicted in the yin-yang symbology, the wolves in the story represent conflicting values. The wolves, the elder tells the young boy, live inside us all, forever engaged in battle. One wolf is evil, angry, envious, sorrowful, greedy, arrogant, resentful, ego-filled and proud; the other is joyful, peaceful, loving, kind, serene, benevolent, empathetic, truthful, generous and faithful. The young boy inevitably asks which wolf will win this eternal struggle, to which the wise man answers, 'The one that you feed'.

Habits are not bad – not at all; without them we would be unable to efficiently navigate the landscapes of our lives. A habit hardwired into our neurology frees up energy and resources for our brains to scan new vistas. Imagine, for example, driving with the aptitude of a beginner: stilted, uncertain and clumsy. Without the power of habit and the skills embedded deep into the circuitry of our brain by practice, an experienced driver would be unable to coordinate driving while simultaneously enjoying the view and chatting with a passenger. Without habit, the driver would remain as ineffective as a beginner for eternity – or at least from London to Brighton!

Habits are self-perpetuating and they shape our decision making; we know what we know and therefore do what we do. For example, if I have inherited the belief that money is the 'root of all evil' – a dark-wolf thought – then my relationship with money and my subsequent choices, habits and life will be markedly different from those of someone who believes that 'good people do good things with money' – the thoughts of an enlightened wolf.

If we foster healthy and positive habits, they will be reflected in our lives. If, however, we repeat the things that cause us pain, we will become masters of our own unhappy demise. To avoid this, as Bruce Lee suggests, it is important to be open to new ways, ways that could lead to new beliefs, thoughts, choices, habits and realities.

In this first part of the book, I will attempt to open your eyes to the idea that money is merely a theoretical construct; an illusion, if you like. I will show that the concept of money is perpetuated, mostly, by inherited beliefs from family and society at large that have formed into hard, unquestioned habit and routine. I will reveal some unsaid truths, burst the bubble of unchallenged 'money myths' and offer some new concepts around the idea of work, life and meaning in a bid to show you that money may not be quite as enslaving as you had assumed.

However, in order to motivate ourselves to change these deep-rooted beliefs and habits, we first need to understand the harm our current relationship with money – a 'money first' attitude – is having on us.

You might notice the tell-tale sign, while lying in bed staring up at the ceiling, or in a quiet moment during your lunch break, or after work, relaxing in the bath following a long day. Anyone might feel it at any moment when there is a pause between busy thoughts. It is the 'Everywhere Nowhere'.

The Everywhere Nowhere is the name I give to the tension that hums in the background of our lives but is almost impossible to pinpoint. It is like a headache or toothache that sits uncomfortably in the periphery, seeming to exist simultaneously both everywhere and nowhere. Buddhists call it 'suffering' or 'unsatisfactoriness' and say that it is the root cause of all our troubles.

Years ago, I noticed it in myself. I had just dropped my two young children off at school and was walking back home thinking about bills and the many things on my 'to-do' list that I needed to complete in order to pay them. As I thought about the day ahead, I realised that my shoulders were tense, my jaw a little clenched and my mood vaguely resentful.

What I really wanted to do, after dropping my children off at school, was to sit down for an hour and write a chapter of the book I had been trying to write for as long as I could remember. What I had to do was rush home quickly and complete the chores before going out to work, teaching tennis for the rest of the afternoon.

The other day I recognised the Everywhere Nowhere in the face of my friend, Simon. We were changing for a morning martial-arts class, and he didn't seem himself. His face was tight with concern and his eyes were weary with rings underneath. With his head in his hands, he admitted that he was reaching the end of his tether. He couldn't bear his long working days. He felt guilty about his feelings because he had only recently landed his dream job. A large corporate had headhunted him and offered him an exciting position in the company, but the novelty was already fading.

Simon hadn't anticipated that the extended working hours that came with his promotion would be so stifling. While celebrating being offered his new position and securing the next rung of success up the career ladder, he had told himself that it would be fine and that he would settle into the new challenges. Besides, he should be happy about his new-found abundance and opportunity, shouldn't he?

It hadn't been fine. He wasn't coping and felt guilty about complaining.

Sheba works in our small local supermarket. She recently graduated from university with a degree in chemistry. Sheba has a warm smile, likes to chat to customers and was excited to tell my wife and me about her latest academic success, while she stacked shelves and we shopped for groceries around her.

The question of what she wanted to do now that she had graduated naturally came up. It was then that I spotted the Everywhere Nowhere in her. It was a sad thing to see in someone not much older than my own daughter.

A little of Sheba's smile faded as she admitted that she didn't know what she wanted to do and would have to keep stacking shelves until she did; her parents had insisted. When I asked her what she would love to do if she didn't need the money, she said she just wanted to sing.

Many of us can relate to this ever-present, subtle tension. It has many causes, but almost always work, money, responsibility and unfulfilled dreams, to some degree, are involved. Yet we push on regardless – either ignoring or denying the problem or simply being too busy to notice.

The Everywhere Nowhere is subtle but insidious. Over time its internal pressure will spill over and affect health, relationships and quality of life. In the UK, just over 107,000 couples divorced in 2016, an increase of 5.8% on the previous year.[1] Historically, according to the Office for National Statistics, many divorce petitions come on the first Monday of the New Year (dubbed 'Divorce day' by lawyers), commonly as a result of concerns over money.

Christmas, meant to be such a happy time, can also be

a great strain, and relationships which are already showing cracks are likely to buckle under the added pressure and expense that it brings. Marriage is not the only casualty of money stress. Health is another.

Emma, a mother of three, admits that following her divorce, it did not take long for the enormous financial stress to affect her health and wellbeing.

'Since the divorce I have become a complete insomniac,' she says. 'I'm just so worried about how I'm going to keep a roof over my children's heads. The antidepressants the doctor has put me on have made me put on a lot of weight and it's hurting my back and my knees – even my hair is falling out. I never feel well anymore and I am increasingly reluctant to leave the house.'

The tragedy of Emma's story is that it is not unique – far from it.

Dr Zoltán Sarnyai, head of the Laboratory of Psychiatric Neuroscience at James Cook University in Australia, explains that stress, whether caused by money or other factors, affects our health by releasing a cascade of potent chemicals, such as adrenalin and cortisol, which increase our heart rate and suppress our immune system.

Evolved over millions of years, these are beneficial chemicals in small doses, as they help fuel a body that might need to escape or contend with immediate danger. However, they become counterproductive in the long term.

'These chemicals are very powerful and need to be

switched off once the [immediate] threat [of danger] is over; otherwise they do damage to the body and the brain', Sarnyai explains.

What Sarnyai is describing is the biology behind the feeling of Everywhere Nowhere, and how it is hurting us. Too much of the wrong sort of stress makes us vulnerable to infection, weight gain and depression, as well as chronic conditions like type 2 diabetes and cancer. If we don't change the way we live, we considerably increase the risk of contracting one of these illnesses.

Beyond health problems, dissatisfaction and divorce, money worries may have an even higher cost.

On 6th January 2014, just two years after becoming a grandmother, Ashley Eneriz's mother decided to drive her car off a 400-foot cliff to her death. It wasn't her first suicide attempt, explained Ashley, and there were several contributory factors to this final decision, but the most prevalent was money. Ashley's mother had become caught in a vicious downward spiral of debt. She saw only one way out.

According to the *British Journal of Psychiatry*, there were over 10,000 'economic suicides' at the peak of the British financial recession between 2008 and 2010.[2] These distressing findings are echoed by an article in the *American Journal of Preventive Medicine*, which reported that during the last fifteen years, financial stress has led to a rise in suicide rates among 40- to 64-year-olds.[3]

Bob, a longtime family friend, was always the life and

soul of a social gathering. It wasn't that he was loud and boisterous, rather the opposite. His gentle manner and warm, genuine smile provided some respite from the loud and boisterous. He was like the party Buddha.

It came as a huge surprise to learn from his distraught wife that Bob was caught and drowning in the money spiral.

Bob had a good position in an IT company based outside London. After the birth of his second child, he decided to take 'garden leave', to enjoy his new daughter and re-evaluate his life. The birth of a child, particularly if you are witness to the delivery, can often be a catalyst for life reorientation.

As baby Sophie grew older, life in the family household returned to normal and Bob's wife naturally started to ask him about his return to work. It was time to get the bills paid.

Refreshed after his rest and the birth of Sophie, Bob dressed for work, picked up his briefcase and headed back to the office. Or so his wife thought.

Six months later, Bob's wife tearfully admitted on the other end of the phone: 'He wasn't going to work at all. He'd kiss us all, leave the house and return at home time, tell me about his day and ask about ours. I thought nothing of it until I opened a couple of late-payment letters from the bank and utility companies. Then I started to feel that something wasn't right. Bob looked haggard and he was always tired and snappy with the kids. It was when

I started to smell alcohol that I knew something more serious was going on.'

Bob had never returned to work on that first day. He had enjoyed his time off with his growing family and it had brought back meaning and context to his life.

Bob is not a religious man, although he was brought up a Catholic, but he refers to himself as a spiritual man, inasmuch as he has always pondered life's big questions: why are we here? Where are we going? What should we be doing with our lives in the meantime?

When it was time to go back to work, he couldn't do it.

'It was like I had seen behind the curtain,' Bob told me. 'The birth of Sophie had made me see, even more than with Enzo [his first child], that life is so much more than going to work and paying bills – the life we are "supposed" to lead. I didn't want to do it any more.'

However, rather than speaking to his wife about how he felt, Bob chose to pretend that he was working until he could figure out a way to meet his financial obligations and live a life he loved. He now realises this was a mistake.

As the illusion continued, the unpaid bills and debts mounted and Bob told me that, fleetingly, he considered suicide. Instead, he turned to drink to temporarily numb the pain rather than end the game permanently.

Happily, Bob's close and extended family provided love, support and money to enable him to pull himself out of his rut. Yet Bob still had to choose to grab the rope, and it was his underlying belief that there is something more to life that finally made him reach out.

Unfortunately, none of these stories is particularly unusual. At some level we know that working to pay the bills kills not only our motivation, but also our bodies, minds and souls – but what are we to do? Debts still need to be paid. We must keep our eyes on the money whether we like it or not. We must sacrifice our ideals to survive in the life and times in which we find ourselves.

Or must we?

It is easy to make assumptions about the world: working hard for money is one of them. But what we see before our eyes, the 'truths' we live by every day, are not always as they seem.

Six people, three wearing black T-shirts and three wearing white, move around in a small group passing two basketballs between them. The instruction to viewers of the video on which they appear is to count the number of times players wearing white pass the basketball. 'The correct answer is fifteen,' the narrator tells us, 'but did you see the gorilla?'

If you've never seen this now infamous test of 'selective attention' by Harvard students Christopher Chabris and Daniel Simons, then you must. (I must confess that I'm about to ruin the effect of it by revealing the results here; so to you, Christopher and Daniel, I'm sorry.*)

---

* As compensation, let me refer readers to another of Chabris and Simons's equally interesting experiments, 'The monkey business illusion' – I promise not to ruin that one.

Most people audibly gasp, as I did, 'What gorilla?' Lo and behold, when the video is played back, this time in slow motion, a person in a gorilla suit does indeed walk straight into the centre of the group of players, beats its chest and walks off out of camera shot.

The conclusion of the experiment is that when we are focused on one thing (in this case counting the passes between the white-T-shirt wearers), we are often blind to other, even outrageously obvious, things.

And this is how we go about living our daily lives. For so long we have focused on the mantras handed down to us from our parents and society – study hard, get a good job, save up and support a family – that we have become blind to other ways of being.

In Buddhism, beliefs that lead to pain and hardship are referred to simply as 'ignorance'. Most of us readily accept that committing to a job that we are ambivalent about, merely to make money, is hardly wise. At best, it causes boredom and dissatisfaction and at worst, depression and anxiety, which can lead to divorce, ill health and even suicide. Yet what are we to do? How can we shift from 'ignorance' to a more 'enlightened' viewpoint? We do so by identifying 'the gorilla in our midst' and then challenging it.

As I mentioned in the introduction, many of the tools we will use to create a life enhanced by meaningful profitable work, are derived from my experiences of Buddhism. They are not exclusively Buddhist tools, just sensible, common-sense methodologies that Buddhists also use. One of these tools is debate.

On its inception over 2,000 years ago, Buddhism had to engage in debate in order to defend and explain its position amid the myriad religions in India at that time. Debate was valued so highly that if you couldn't defend your position and lost the debate, you were compelled to convert to the view of your opponent.

This 'question everything' attitude is one of the unique strengths of Buddhism to this day and something that we can all use to our advantage. It means we don't have to follow blindly doctrines of religion, science, philosophy or new-age fads, none of which have a monopoly on 'ultimate truth'. Instead, we can form our own view of life based on our unique findings.

With this in mind, this first chapter's goal has been to help you see that your 'money first' attitude is causing you pain. I have shown you that there is a gorilla in the room and that you are not alone in failing to spot it. My next task is to identify the roots of the belief system that causes the pain, so that we may challenge its validity.

Once the stranglehold of a 'money first' belief has been shaken loose, you will be better motivated and more open to new ways of being; ways that can lead you to a working life about which you are passionate and which still pays the bills.

Let us move on to the next chapter, to find out how the concept of money came to be.

Money makes the world go round

The 'money first' paradigm

How did money and all the worries that come with it become so central to our lives? Was it always this way? Is this the only relationship we can have with money?

Some paradigms are so well established within societies that they become accepted 'facts' when, in truth, they are little more than unchallenged beliefs. The paradigm of 'money makes the world go around' is one example.

It is a paradigm that leads us to prioritise the accumulation of money so that we may afford our dreams and desires. Without money, we believe, our goals will remain unrealised, marooned between our ears as thoughts, little more than hopes. That's why so many people remain in jobs they don't care about. Our futures are at the mercy of our bank accounts.

In any toxic relationship, both parties hold responsibility for their own role and reaction; the acceptance of this truth arms us to tackle the problem. By accepting our part in the dysfunctional relationship between ourselves and the money industry, we are empowered by the reality that we are free to investigate and choose other ways of thinking. We can step away from the tyranny, even if it might be a difficult challenge.

The early days

Since it came into being as an idea some 11,000 years ago, money has morphed, uncontested, into a 'thing' as real as a table or chair. But it hasn't always been this way. So, what happened before the concept of money?

Our early hunter-gatherer ancestors not only survived without money, they coped well enough to evolve into the modern humans we are today. Early humans developed a varied set of skills and talents to meet their own personal needs and those of their community. It was Nature, with all the attendant pressures on humans to survive her, and not the demands of a commercial marketplace, that determined what people needed to do to live to see another day. 'Invisible currencies' such as communal reciprocity and skill sharing were used, not for future profit, but for the immediate survival of both the individual and the community.

Survival and security are at the base of a theoretical model called the 'Hierarchy of Needs' proposed by Abraham Maslow, one of the most influential psychologists of the twentieth century. Maslow wrote about his model in 1943, as part of an academic paper entitled 'A Theory of Human Motivation'.

The theory describes five layers of need, depicted as levels rising up a pyramid. At the base of the pyramid are the physiological needs such as air for breathing, water, food, sleep, clothing and shelter. Rising up the pyramid are safety needs: family morality and health, protection of the body, property and resources; followed by emotional and social needs: love and a sense of belonging, friendship, family and sexual intimacy. Next come the needs of the self: self-esteem, confidence, achievement, respect for and from others; and finally self-actualisation: morality, creativity, spontaneity, problem solving and lack of prejudice.

Our early ancestors successfully scaled the 'Hierarchy of Needs' model without being reliant on money. And as they developed their survival skills, communities grew, with more people needing to meet Maslow's hierarchical model. And as demand for food, shelter, security and confidence increased, the providers of skills became specialists.

Nature, and all her unpredictability, would always remain at the helm of life, however. At any moment, the subtle balancing act required for staying alive could be thrown into disarray by a change in the weather, a plague of insects or an epidemic of disease. A drought would cause an increase in demand for the water diviners in the community, while those producing winter clothing could find themselves suddenly twiddling their thumbs.

From barter to money

Changes in availability, whether surplus or dearth, alter demand. And the increasing complexities brought about by increasing populations engendered a desire for other systems of trade. Thus the concept of barter was born.

Barter can only work successfully if those doing the bartering need something that others have to offer and they in turn have what others require. If, for example, a gardener needs some new gardening shoes and the cobbler needs his hedged trimmed, they are in luck. However, if the cobbler has a paved garden and would instead prefer a pot of herbal ointment for his chapped hands, the bartering deal becomes more intricate: the gardener and the cobbler must search for a herbalist in need of their skills. The solution to these intricacies is money.

Let's take a whistle-stop tour through the chronological history of money to better understand how we came to arrive at a 'money first' attitude.

- Early records show that in Egypt, around 9000 BC, early humans bartered for goods they needed with products they had in surplus. Non-perishable goods such as grain and cattle were suitable barter commodities.
- By 1100 BC, in China, bronze was used to fashion miniature sculptures to be offered as an alternative currency of barter – it was easier to carry small

bronze items in your pocket than move around with cows or sacks of grain. Around the same time, 1200 BC, a further refinement saw these sculptures develop into rounded coins. In some coastal regions around the Indian Ocean, communities used the local cowrie shells as another form of currency.

- In 600 BC, King Alyattes of Lydia (modern-day Turkey) minted the first official currency, thus standardising coinage and facilitating overseas trade.

- In AD 1250, the Florentines, not wishing to be outdone by the Lydians, minted their own gold coin, which became the accepted currency across Europe.

- As trade evolved, the search was on for a solution to the problem of transporting international currency, as shipping large chests of silver and gold was both cumbersome and costly. Sweden found the answer in paper money in 1661, although it took some time for this to gain widespread acceptance – old habits die hard and pirates still preferred their chests of loot.

- In 1860, the American company Western Union established itself as the market leader in all matters of money, and the company spearheaded e-money with the novel idea of transferring it electronically via telegram.

- In 1946, the game of money evolved again when an American businessman, John Biggins, invented the credit card by introducing his 'Charg-It' card.

- 1999 saw European banks keeping up progress by offering mobile phone banking and a common European currency, the euro, came into circulation in 2002.

- In 2008, contactless payments were introduced in the UK for the first time.

- From 2014 onwards, new forms of currency appeared, some successful and promising, others merely fads or mistakes: cryptocurrencies such as bitcoin; modern barter systems like Bartercard; evolved versions of contactless banking, like Apple Pay and wearable wristbands.

In his book *Sapiens: A Brief History of Humankind*, professor, author and historian Yuval Noah Harari writes: 'Money was created many times in many places. Its development required no technological breakthroughs – it was a purely mental revolution. It involved the creation of a new inter-subjective reality that exists solely in people's shared imagination.'[4]

Consider Harari's statement carefully. Money is a mental construct, an act of imagination, an agreed tool of make-believe, made up to solve the burgeoning problems of early traders. It is not a universal law or truth. It is not, as we imagine, as real as it seems.

Money is a fascinating concept. No other single development in history, apart from religion, has had such an enslaving and controlling force over humans. Yet money has no intrinsic material value; it is merely an invention designed to represent the abstract and invisible as something tangible and concrete.

This piece of Native American wisdom speaks volumes about the illusion of money: 'When the last tree is cut, the last fish is caught, and the last river is polluted; when to breathe the air is sickening, you will realise, too late, that wealth is not in bank accounts and that you can't eat money.'

The sleight of hand involved in the invention of money making something seem real when it is not, could only occur to begin with thanks to a voluntary cooperation between parties, and only persists today because of our ignorance of the shackles money places around our ankles.

Despite having no innate value, every single day money manages to turn 'land into loyalty, justice to health and violence into knowledge. With money as a go-between, any two people can cooperate on any project,' Harari says.

Money works because we are prepared to agree on the value of a chosen symbol (coins, silver ingots, cigarettes or whatever) – an illusion perpetuated by trust or wilful ignorance, depending on your viewpoint.

Examine a dollar bill, and you will see the words 'In God we trust'. The words could read instead: 'In our neighbours we trust, to pay the value of this bill for goods or services on whose value we have also agreed.' Wordy. 'In God we trust' fits better.

The mention of God on monetary bills raises yet another point. Religion is also an imagined concept with no inherent value. The value is derived from groups trusting in each other's 'story' and agreeing on what that story is worth.

We have to agree that a bar of chocolate costs 90 pence just as we have to accept that our religion upholds kindness and the eradication of sin. It is we humans, and no one else, who decide both of these points. There are no specific universal laws governing the cost of a bar of chocolate or what constitutes correct religious behaviour.

Although both religion and money are equally lacking in innate value, it is money that has won the game of universal acceptability. A Muslim would not be welcome to recite the Koran during the Lord's Prayer, but donations to the collection plate are welcome whatever the religious denomination. We can reject one part of a person's make-believe while simultaneously embracing the other. 'Money is the most universal and most efficient system of mutual trust ever devised,' Harari observes.

The fact that people all over the world can be united by trust in the idea of money, but be torn apart by religious beliefs is because, ultimately, money is exchanged for those goods and services that Nature has determined we need to survive; the physiological needs described by Maslow. Whereas we can reject someone's religious ideology because it is not likely to kill us (although their subsequent decision to become a warmonger might).

Lazy money

This understanding raises yet another idea that we need to explore. For this, I want you to imagine an apocalyptic world. All money has been burned, and smoke rises from the ash pile into the sky, which remains untroubled despite the destruction below. The wind will continue to blow, and the rains will come, as they always have. Life will do its best, as it always does, to clamber through death, and slight movements in surrounding bushes suggest that there have indeed been survivors.

Those few survivors will return as hunter-gatherers. No longer will they have money, for it lies smouldering in the ash pile, and the infrastructure that wealth supported has ground to a halt. Yet, without it all, they will live to see another day. How? Because Nature will take their hand, as it always has, and it will lead them back to their inherent drive for survival. There is more to life than money.

This apocalyptic example should help us to keep money in perspective, but it is not a mode of thinking that many employ. Instead, we delve ever deeper into the rabbit hole of money. Our ever increasing reliance on money prevents us from questioning its reality, and it is this blindness that creates the nine-to-five treadmill of bills, deadlines and material gain above and beyond our needs. This is one of the big causes of the pain we feel through the Everywhere Nowhere.

Our belief in money has made us lazy in many ways. Money is just one means of getting what we need, but it is not the only means to this end and by relying solely on the concept of money, our creativity, faith and trust in the value of the natural abilities within ourselves and our interdependent communities have become flaccid through under-use.

When we believe that money is something more important than a convenient symbol of exchange, we might, for example, find ourselves mindlessly giving a homeless person an off-the-cuff ten-pound donation rather than taking the time to speak to him, one human being to another, a simple yet powerful act often overlooked by those of us who think money is a cure-all.

As our habitual, unchallenged, 'money first' attitude deepens and becomes rooted in the next generation, it is not uncommon for children to believe that the fruits and vegetables they eat are produced in 'the supermarket' rather than by farmers in fields. This dissociation from the raw source of all that money buys would be funny if it weren't so painfully true! And the dissociation doesn't stop there.

Once we unquestioningly buy into the idea that money makes the world go round and that, with enough of it, our lives will be complete, we focus single-mindedly on the accumulation of wealth. Money becomes our master, our new God and religion. We stop looking to the heavens for meaning and answers to life's questions; instead we search inside our wallets. We stop meeting up with our friends, family and community to commune and muse existentially, whether in a place of worship or not, instead we extend our work hours – 'open all weekend' is good for profits, after all.

When it all comes crashing down, and we either lose what money we have gained or die before enjoying it, or indeed are never fortunate enough to enjoy financial wealth in the first place, then we are left feeling utterly useless and destitute.

Increasing numbers of studies link poverty with the strategic economic slavery of capitalism; but capitalism can only control us if we continue to buy into the idea that money is the sole creator and provider of our futures and the most dominant indicator of success.

Poverty is not just a problem of money: it is a problem resulting from a lack of faith in our creativity and in our natural and personal resources, those that existed long before money and which will remain long after.

So the question is: if you knew that all of your needs would be met without money, would it change the way you live? If you knew that your desires would be satisfied, one way or another, irrespective of money, would you be a little more relaxed about life? In this book I will suggest that this can, and does, happen.

Some years ago, I was inspired by the book *One Red Paperclip*, written by Kyle MacDonald. MacDonald wanted a house. The problem was he didn't have a job and he didn't have any money. By modern monetary values Kyle MacDonald was 'poor'.

The book goes on to tell the story of how he started out with a red paperclip that was holding together the pages of his CV, and traded it 'upward' for something of slightly more value – a pen shaped like a fish, which he then traded for a doorknob – and on it went. To cut an inspiring story short, he ends up with a house, all garnered from a series of trades starting from 'one red paperclip'.

His story is a wonderful example of not just human creativity and resourcefulness, but also the invisible currencies that exist. Yet we are not taught about these types of currencies in our schools even though there are plenty of them. Part of the reason for this lies in the difficulty of measuring them.

We tend to believe in what we can see, measure and prove; it is a consequence of the scientific method that pervades our modern world. While I'm not encouraging the type of blind, ignorant faith that can lead to extremism and cult-likeworship, I would suggest that not all things need to be seen to be believed. Sometimes you may have to 'believe before you see', to borrow a line from the late, great spiritual writer Dr Wayne Dyer.

Here is another example of invisible currencies in action. On the 14th June 2017, I left the city of Nottingham very early (4.30am) to beat the rush-hour traffic that would soon clog the roads leading into London. This, though, would prove to be more than just another working day in the capital – it was a day that will be indelibly scarred into the memories of both the victims and the witnesses of one of the worst disasters in the UK since the Second World War: the Grenfell fire tragedy.

Approaching London on the M1 motorway I noticed what I first thought were storm clouds – black and grey swirls dirtying the otherwise perfectly blue early-morning sky. Only later did I realise that they were smoke clouds still billowing from the Grenfell tower block that had been ignited five hours previously.

Seventy two people died and more than 70 were injured in the fire. For the 223 people who escaped the blaze, life would need to be rebuilt amid the loss, trauma and grief.

Many who had lived in the tower were on the lower end of the income spectrum, and their whole material lives had burned with their flats. Without disposable income, savings or extended family many of the residents wondered if the streets might be their next home.

As tragic as the Grenfell tragedy most certainly is, it is also indicative of the hope, faith, community – all invisible currencies – that are often created out of the flames of adversity.

The martial arts academy where I exercise several times a week looks out over the Grenfell Tower. And in the days and weeks that followed the fire, I was extremely moved to witness a truly amazing display of compassion and interdependent cooperation in aid of the Grenfell victims by men and women of all ages, races, faiths and economic means.

Donations of clothes, food, toiletries and essentials filled makeshift distribution centres; people offered their homes to strangers; others knitted blankets and new toys for children; groups set up soup kitchens; many others offered love, support and a shoulder to cry on. The community launched into action, for the benefit of their neighbours, way ahead of government agencies mobilising more formal methods of aid.

Local people gave whatever they could muster; some of them money, mostly not. Invisible currencies abounded.

At the foot of the tower, now irrevocably damaged by the smoke, was the Dale Youth Boxing Club, a boxing gym that had served the youth of the community for close to twenty years. While the gym had developed some high-level boxing superstars over the years (James DeGale, George Groves and Daniel Dubois), its true value lay in the untold stories of young people it had saved over the years from with the risk of criminality, all too often the narrative of inner-city life.

The loss of the gym to the community was more than money could measure, but it was money, and a great deal of it, that would be needed to restore this vital asset back to them. Who would invest in such a place?

Invisible currencies do not just fund the small things like knitted jumpers, cans of food, duvets or pillows; invisible currencies have enough weight to fund big projects too.

DIY SOS is a BBC television programme in which a team of builders carry out a building project for a worthwhile cause. They rely solely on donated material from local businesses and the physical efforts of volunteers from the surrounding community. In its largest project to date, it chose the rebuilding of the Dale Youth Boxing gym at Grenfell as its worthwhile project.

In a local newspaper, *DIY SOS* presenter Nick Knowles branded the boxing gym project as the most ambitious in the show's history. The nonstop nine-week build cost over £2 million in donations to complete; everyone, including the survivors, it seemed, doubted that the power of invisible currency could stretch into the millions. But it did, and the gym has been rebuilt and equipped to a state-of-the-art design, and includes a new community centre and space where residents and survivors of the fire can go to get counselling if they wish.

It would be facile to suggest that money doesn't play a part – a big part – in our world; of course it does, but our reliance on money as the *only means* of exchange is equally facile and lazy. Community, interdependent help and cooperation, donations, invention, creativity and, yes, sometimes, a divine hand that we cannot see but whose effect we can feel, are all valuable types of currency above and beyond cash.

The time and money trap

There is yet another problem with the 'money first'

paradigm: although in theory money is an infinite resource, depending on the size of your imagination and the tactics employed in making it, Nature is always there to throw a spanner in the works. That spanner is time.

No matter how focused you are on the goal of money, no matter how much you celebrate its gains, mourn its losses and believe in its role as the axis of the world, there is a ticking bomb waiting to explode. From the moment that we are born, sooner or later, we are doomed to die. Nature says so, and no one has yet proved her wrong. Time supersedes all artificial monetary laws by merely stopping the game once it has had enough.

This countdown to our end, however, seems to have accentuated our obsession with money, rather than put it in perspective. Rather than wake up and let go of this conceptual prison that we have built around ourselves, we push harder into the game and try to amass more and more before the bell tolls our death. Money is no longer just a means to the end goal of exchange for the essential goods and services that keep us alive – it has become both the means and the end. Today we live in a world where money makes money via the influence of the banking industry (more of this in the next chapter) and we have allowed money to become indicative of our worth.

But when and why did money change from being an extended means of barter into the behemothic headache it is today? When did it become the primary mission of our lives, a mission that so many of us accept unquestioningly?

When did our self-worth and value become so inextricably linked to money? It is difficult to know for sure but I would like to suggest that it was the moment when we began to equate money with power.

For generations we have watched the 'king in his counting house, counting all his money' and naturally, if not mistakenly, associated money with power. Who, after all, doesn't want power, the energy that fuels the survival skills of the fittest? In fact, neither the king nor his money are the real source of power – for that we must look elsewhere – and later we will. His power, like his money, is an illusion. No amount of money can give a king natural power, just as the alpha status of a wolf pack cannot be bought by the runt of the litter.

But we have observed that the king has all the riches – all the material riches – and the weight of an army to enforce his law and have assumed that money is the key to success. This is the greatest misunderstanding of human thought.

As some of us, hypnotised by the shimmering gold of the king's crown, dived head first into the accumulation of wealth to slake our thirst for self-worth, canny others decided to exploit and capitalise on our insecurities. These are the players of the game of money. It is a game where the winner has accumulated the most. A game where the champion is decided, not by those who score the most goals, tries or points, but by those with the most pounds and pence. It is these people who have led us further into the rabbit hole of finance. We have fallen for their promises, cowered from their fear-mongering and been bamboozled by their small print. They are the bankers – that amorphous group who play us like pawns and are rewarded by our losses.

Whatever our personal drive to make more money, we must consider the behaviour of these conjurors of currency so that we may better understand how we became ensnared in their game. Only then can we consider how to unlock ourselves from their chains, live autonomously and create a future of our own making.

Money and the banking sector

'Get your money for nothing and your
chicks for free.'

         – Dire Straits

Humans like to push beyond boundaries; it is one of the benefits of an evolved consciousness: the ability to self-reflect and strive. However, this comes at a price. With the ability to desire whatever may be waiting in greener pastures comes the habit of dreaming up myriad inventions by which to achieve it, good or bad, kind or cunning. Our beautiful minds are a double-edged weapon that we carry with us throughout our time on earth.

Any parent can attest to a time when they have told their toddler 'no', only to watch the chastised child not only continue the forbidden behaviour but do so while looking them straight in the eye with a wry smile. The banking industry, with which this chapter is concerned, is another disobedient, rule-stretching 'naughty child'.

Banking has capitalised on our unwillingness to challenge the paradigm of money and has built a global industry so powerful that it is difficult to escape even if we wanted to – difficult, but not impossible.

Banking is a game. It is a game of money-making-money for money's sake. The tactics and techniques of the banking sector fall outside the remit of this book, primarily because we will not be subscribing to its rules. Suffice to say that banking is the ultimate illusionist.

In essence, banking is the practice of making money from selling something that doesn't exist, has no inherent value and certainly will not help us survive our hypothetical apocalypse.

Think about that for a moment. Nothing from nature is exchanged through banking: nothing tangible or real anyway. The industry is held up by illusion, a perverse kind of trust and the reliance on no one questioning the reality. More often than not, it takes the crashing surprise of an economic depression to reveal the truth behind the game.

But when did we start to treat money as an overarching universal law? Michael Taylor is the 'Anonymous Banker'[5]. Via his website, Taylor teaches people about money and finance and he shows them how to see through the smoke-screen of the financial sector's secretive and confusing vernacular. Taylor became a high-flying American banker after graduating from Harvard. Like many others in the industry, he climbed the ranks through study, hard work, competitive ambition and a sprinkling of serendipity. He lists running a private investment limited partnership and selling bonds in the mortgage and emerging markets departments of Goldman Sachs among his achievements in money game.

The Everywhere Nowhere niggled away at Taylor until he was forced to make a change. Despite his success in the financial sector, he left it to teach.

'I'm not really anonymous, I just liked the thematic idea of "getting sober", about money and finance,' Taylor says. 'I founded Bankers Anonymous because, as a recovering banker, I believe that the gap between the financial world, as I know it, and the public discourse about finance is more than just a problem for a family trying to balance their cheque book, or politicians trying to score points over next year's budget – it is a weakness of our civil society.'

I asked Taylor when and how he thought the change came from money being used as a means to an end (my two chickens in exchange for your bale of straw), to being both the means and the end.

'That's a big question and I don't have any formulated answer,' he admits, 'but it does make me think of something I was reading last night to my eight-year-old daughter, from the book *The Little House on the Prairie*.

'In the chapter we are reading, the characters are on the prairie – they're probably somewhere between 40 and 100 miles from any other European-descended settlers.

There might be Indians in the area, but they don't know. And there's a lovely description – it's quite meditative actually – of the birds, the prairies, the animals and the stars. The rest of the chapter is essentially meditations on washing the petticoats and setting up and warming up food on the fire.

'But there's no money to be seen: who would you buy from? They have nothing to trade... yet they survive and survive well. They fetch water and wash their clothes further upstream, they kill and eat the prairie rabbits and use the fur to keep warm, and they play in the long grass then harvest it to make thatch.

'So, in answer to your question, as recently as the nineteenth century, at least in this semi-fictional telling, it was possible to survive without money.'

Two thoughts

Considering further the question of when and why money became both the means and the end, my conversation with Taylor turned from literature to history. 'Thinking about it,' he said, 'I suspect that in reality the need for money, and accumulating surplus money, comes from the sovereign with their taxation demands, wherein the regular people must honour a debt to a centralised authority.'

Taylor makes a good point, for as far back as records began, leaders, sovereigns, tsars, shoguns, tribal chiefs and all manner of head honchos have demanded taxes.

At best, the return to the taxpayer would often be little more than a token gesture of reciprocity – of less value, illusory value, or no value at all. More heinous leaders would skip the pretence altogether and simply take taxes in return for the taxpayer's life. Slightly more politically correct leaders, to save face, might spin the tax benefits as 'protection', or promise to hold the payer in 'high favour' with government, or offer other equally empty benefits.

It is not unreasonable to suggest that these early attitudes towards taxation have paved the way for the game of money that we see today in the global banking sectors and insurance industries.

Selina Lamy has worked at Citibank for over fifteen years and knows the world of finance well. I asked Selina the same question I asked Taylor: why did banking become the game it is today?

'Greed,' she finally admitted, after taking time to search for a less damning word. Insight from an insider.

Whether it is breaking the four-minute mile, walking on the moon, splitting the atom or making a million pounds, humans love to strive and improve. We love to play, and if possible, to win.

The game of money is about the love of accumulating wealth. It is no longer simply the medium for the provision of things that Maslow depicted in his pyramid of needs. In itself, this idea is not problematic. Playing a game, whatever the end prize, is every human's prerogative. It only becomes a problem if it affects those not choosing or wanting to play, or worse, those who don't know that they are playing in the first place.

Arnold Swarzennegger's head atop the tracks of a miniature tank, warning shoppers not to miss the PPI compensation deadline, might well be the most bizarre 60 seconds of British television advertising ever filmed. But its airing on prime-time TV is testimony to how many 'regular' people were unknowingly affected by the PPI scandal.

PPI stands for Payment Protection Insurance. Since the 1990s, banks have sold these types of insurance policies alongside mortgages, loans and credit cards. They were designed to repay people's borrowings in situations where they could no longer keep up repayments: through job loss, illness or other unavoidable circumstances. On paper the concept of PPI appeared sensible and fair; the reality was less altruistic.

In 2004, *The Guardian* revealed that many banks were returning just 15% of their PPI claim to claimants, making PPI more lucrative to the banks than car and home insurance.[6] With this in mind, the banks aggressively pursued sales.

In 2008, the PPI scandal escalated after *Which?*, the consumer magazine, reported that one in three PPI customers had been sold 'worthless' insurance. Consumers had been pawns in a profligate, yet profitable banking game of which they knew nothing. Most people had very little idea that they were even buying PPI, and even fewer knew that they had any choice in the matter.

Behind the curtain

Dressed in white jumpsuits and wearing box-fresh white sneakers, three men wheel a raised platform up against the Great Wall of China. On it is the frame of a large metal box, with stairs leading down from it to the ground. A tall, handsome man all dressed in black, except for a white towel draped around his shoulders, slowly and deliberately walks up the steps and into the box.

He reaches out to touch the Great Wall, as if caressing a long-time love that he hasn't seen for some time, and feels the giant stones at his fingertips. As he considers the wall, the men in white join him on the platform and two of them unroll white cloths to create fabric sides for the metal box, while the third, once the curtains are fully secured in place, turns on a spotlight to reveal the silhouette of the man in black.

That man was David Copperfield, the world-famous illusionist of the 1980s, and he was about to walk through the Great Wall of China.

I remember sitting around the TV with my family, spellbound by this seemingly impossible feat of magic.

Copperfield, now in his late sixties, is still wowing audiences with his show in a theatre in a Las Vegas hotel. People flock to see his illusions, and although they know full well the sleight of hand involved, they suspend their disbelief in order to be entertained. It is a human trait: to employ wilful blindness if, in one way or another, it serves us to do so.

The way out of the hotel, following Copperfield's show, (strategically chosen by the hotel designers and owners, not Copperfield himself, I presume) weaves a course past the bright lights of the slot machines, the spinning wheels of the roulette tables and the charming smiles of the men and woman waiting to serve. To this den of iniquity, everyday folk flock and suspend their common sense to engage, trance-like, in the game of gambling.

Wilful blindness is used by all of us in all manner of circumstances, not least in regard to our finances. In the case of PPI and other types of insurance, the motivation for our blindness is fear of an uncertain future; with gambling, it is the same, but tinged with a perverse type of hope, that the future might be brighter. Both states of mind, fear and hope, often prevent us from looking behind the curtain for the truth of the reality just beyond our sight.

However, our financial lives are not a game. Our blindness is affecting us, and our wilful ignorance is ruining us, financially, mentally, emotionally, physically and spiritually.

It is our responsibility to look behind the curtain, question the reality and begin playing by a new set of rules; rules that are loaded in our favour. I hope these early chapters are assisting you to assume this responsibility.

Surplus and the natural world

In the natural world, rules of artifice can never be our

saviour, because they don't work there. Nature has her own unavoidable set of rules and guidelines.

My wife is South African. She loves to reminisce about childhood camping holidays with her family in neighbouring Botswana. She remembers helping pack to the brim an old, green army Land Rover with camping gear; enough for her and her family to survive for three weeks in the Botswana bush. Her eyes sparkle when she remembers looking up at the stars with a campfire crackling nearby.

Although today Botswana is more developed and tourist ridden than in the days of my wife's 1970s holidays, it is still one of the last bastions of unspoiled nature left in Africa. As a Londoner, I was awestruck when she first took me. At last I understood what she meant when she referred to that 'sense of "bigness" you only get in the bush'.

It was in Botswana that I first saw lions in the wild, rather than in a picture book or behind the glass walls of London Zoo. There is something transcendent about nature, particularly the raw (every pun intended) unfiltered essence of a predator such as a lion.

You can feel the guttural gulp and roar of a male lion deep in the pit of your stomach, and it activates a fear for survival in the brain that is entwined in the DNA inherited from our hunter-gatherer ancestors. A lion's roar quickly puts you back in touch with Nature's laws.

Two things strike me whenever I visit the Botswana bush: how superfluous the non-natural world is and how

Nature does not deal in excess. It doesn't work harder than is necessary; trees don't focus to grow, flowers don't set ambitious targets, and flocks of starlings don't meet regularly to discuss tactics and training in the intricacies of murmuration.

Nature isn't greedy. While there are exceptions to every rule, mostly, Nature does not take, or give, more than is needed.

It is important at this stage to acknowledge the phenomenon known as 'Henhouse Syndrome'. It is a term invented by Dutch biologist Hans Kruuk after he studied hyenas in Africa and red foxes in England.[7]

Kruuk observed that some animals do indeed engage in the behaviour of surplus killing – these include zooplankton, damselfly naiads, predaceous mites, martens, weasels, honey badgers, wolves, orcas, red foxes, leopards, lions, spotted hyenas, spiders, brown bears, American black bears, polar bears, coyotes, lynxes, minks, raccoons, dogs, house cats and, of course, humans.

The question, then, is not so much whether surplus-driven behaviour exists in both the natural and human world, as about the motivation and degrees of such behaviour.

Even in the cases where long-term food storage was not the motivation, Kruuk's researchers found that surplus killing still served a role in terms of ongoing survival; such as procuring food for offspring or to gain, or teach, valuable killing skills.

It would be naïve to suggest that it is only humans that break the natural laws of the world. I have witnessed, first hand, a young elephant wilfully stamping a cactus tree to smithereens just, as the wildlife guide said, 'for the hell of it'! But it's humans, with our incessant need for more and more, that have stretched the boundaries and pushed our planet to the edge of extinction. It is the uniquely human trait of attaching self-worth to money that has fuelled the desire for never-ending growth.

Beyond greed, another motivation for the accumulation of money beyond our direct and obvious needs is fear. The phrase 'saving for a rainy day' reveals all that we need to know about fear and money – our unspoken, but primary anxiety – that at some future time there will not be enough to meet our requirements, so we should take more than we need, right now – just in case.

Savings, bonds, pensions and the like are all tinged with the threat of being without money, and, on the surface at least, seem like pretty good investments. We teach our children to save rather than squander and to budget rather than to blow it all. While sensible, living a life against a subtle backdrop of fear is hardly inspiring, and although people have hoarded and saved for generations, it is not a natural process, nor, I would argue, a happy one.

To return once again to our hypothetical question of the previous chapter: if you knew that all of your needs would be met, whenever you needed them, would you waste your life chasing money?

Who, though, or what would provide for your needs?

It is time to search for the source of these abundant natural gifts depicted in the chapters of *The Little House on the Prairie* that Michael Taylor reads to his daughter.

Part II

The Path of Meaning

The search for meaning

Now that we have seen behind the curtain that hides the truth about the illusory nature of money, our faith in its all-encompassing importance may begin to destabilise. Good. In the absence of certainty, we are forced to look elsewhere for meaning and guidance.

The sound of silence

There is something that is present inside all of us, even if we are not always conscious of it.

We might feel it when lying in a field on a lazy summer afternoon, looking up at the banks of white clouds morphing from one shape into another; first a heart, then a giraffe's head, and if we squint one eye, we might make out a section of the Eiffel Tower. Or when staring into a campfire, mesmerised by the flames, the pop and crackle of burning wood and the twisting and twirling trails of smoke. Sometimes we might feel it while looking out to sea towards the horizon with the natural soundtrack of rhythmic waves crashing against the shore.

It is always there, but it is in moments free from distraction, thought and chore that the sound of silence resonates most deeply for us. In those moments we are experiencing the 'unnamable thing', the life force at our centre, from which the daily narratives of humanity play out.

It is the blank canvas at our core waiting for us to paint onto it whatever we care to imagine. It is capable of holding all of our creations, good, bad and indifferent, and can be wiped clean and redrawn, or left and admired. It is in this source of all life, a source above and beyond any laws of finance, one that will survive an apocalypse, where answers to a rich and meaningful existence can be found.

The meaning of life

Since the dawn of time, humans have searched for the meaning of life. Not to search is impossible. It is a quality of an evolved consciousness. Humans ask themselves all manner of questions to understand and confirm their place in the order of things.

It is only natural to want to understand and embrace that to which, we know, intuitively, we are connected. Gazing up at the stars we ask the questions: why are we here? Where do we go after we die? What should we be doing while we are here? Who is in control, us or something else? At one time or another, we have all pondered on (or will ponder on) these types of questions.

With the search for meaning come answers, insights, theories and hypotheses. From the beginning of history these ideas were collected and, to a greater or lesser extent, systematised so that they could be taught to future generations.

Stories told around the campfire became cultural myths and legend, all with lessons to teach and be learned. Later, as knowledge, insight and theories evolved, three distinct systems of enquiry, doctrine and education emerged: religion, philosophy and science. Within each system myriad schools of thought formed with their own nuanced views, opinions and findings on the central theme.

No matter how evolved or grandiose these systems become, ultimately, they are grounded in the search for the meaning of life; united by the unnamable and unfathomable mystery of it all.

Let's briefly look at the three main systems.

Religion

All religions, including the major ones such as Christianity, Islam, Hinduism, Buddhism, Sikhism, Judaism, Confucianism, Jainism advocate the belief in a supernatural power or powers (God, gods, deities and the like), which they regard as both the creators and the governors of the universe. Whether they are monotheistic – believing in one central ruling god – or polytheistic

– believing in many gods and deities – the central idea of religion is that there is a big boss that humans are obliged to appease in order to secure a favourable life and afterlife.

Although religion abdicates much responsibility for life's direction to the divine, the art of prayer and the following of religious tenets allow humans to have some say in the shaping of their future, if only through the benevolence of a well-appeased God.

Philosophy

The word philosophy means 'the love of wisdom' in Greek and, according to the *American Heritage Dictionary*, wisdom is defined as 'the ability to discern or judge what is true, right, or lasting'.[8]

Philosophers value education and thinking. They investigate both the internal and external landscape of humans in order to discover what is true. They aim to harmonise both the inner and outer experience. They are open-minded testers of experience, taking nothing for granted, or on blind faith (as religion might), yet neither rejecting the possibility of the supernatural.

Immanuel Kant, one of the great German philosophers, summarises philosophy beautifully: 'Two things fill me with constantly increasing admiration and awe, the longer and more earnestly I reflect on them: the starry heavens without, and the Moral Law within.'

Science

While religion looked up to the heavens, and philosophy looked within and around, science sought a defining method to prove objectively, or disprove, life's mysteries, or at least those right before our eyes (and the other four senses). The scientific method has six (sometimes seven) steps:

1. Ask a question to which you want answers.
2. Do research to find the answers.
3. Propose a hypothesis based on this research – a kind of educated guess at the answer.
4. Experiment and test the validity of your hypothesis, without cheating or manipulating the findings to fit your beliefs.
5. Record and analyse your findings and discoveries and compare them against your hypothesis.
6. Draw a conclusion that will either prove, or disprove, your original hypothesis.
7. Rinse and repeat with a new question.

Where religion is prepared to believe, science wants proof, but the very tool science wields also limits it. Man-made instruments can only test so far: a machine can record the effect on a crash test dummy of a car colliding at 30 miles an hour, but it is not so easy to measure our mental, spiritual or metaphysical terrains.

Carl Jung (1875–1961), the famous Swiss psychiatrist, psychoanalyst and founder of analytical psychology, recognises the limitations of a purely science-based route to discovery: 'Science is the tool of the Western mind and with it more doors can be opened than with bare hands. It is part and parcel of our knowledge and *obscures our insight only when it holds that the understanding given by it is the only kind there is.*' [my italics]

Although each of these three pioneering systems of truth exploration has limitations, we owe them a great deal. It is these systems – religion, philosophy and science – that have paved the way to today's nuanced, if incomplete, understanding of life. Today, many of us look to a variety of sources to help face life's challenges, rather than just one; this book is an example.

If you meet the Buddha, kill him

Buddhism, one of the major religious-belief systems, is a source of inspiration to which many look for life answers.

It is a unique religion in that it sits equally well among the holy, the philosophical, the scientific and the man and woman on the street.

Many of the lessons of Buddhism are not strictly religious, but rather 'humanist'. Commitment to the religion itself is not necessary in order to benefit from much of its wisdom. Of course, as a religion, Buddhism has great depths that its adherents are free to explore, but this is not a book about Buddhism so much as one inspired by it.

What I have learned, from over 25 years' practice of Buddhism, and in particular my experiences while walking a Buddhist pilgrimage in Japan, can most certainly help.

A favourite Buddhist phrase of mine is: 'If you meet the Buddha, kill him!' When I first heard it, I was a little shocked and confused. It didn't seem to sit well with the peaceful and compassionate teachings that I had understood to be an integral part of Buddhist practice. Over the years, as I pondered the phrase more and more, I realised that it is a call not to anarchy, but to action.

Buddhism insists that followers do not follow Buddhist instruction blindly but, instead, test everything they hear for themselves (as do the philosophers and scientists).

Metaphorical Buddha killing encourages people to reject the unquestioned faith that has dogged so many religions and cults of the past. Rather than placing reliance on a guru, leader or 'higher power', Buddhism advocates self-study, research and experiential discovery. Buddhism is a system of doing, rather than merely listening or blindly following.

Following the crowd and approaching life theoretically rather than experientially is not uncommon; arguably more of us live as 'cerebral sheep' than the 'free-will pioneers' we imagine ourselves to be.

There are reasons why we tread the road most travelled. For evolutionary survival, it is safer to be part of a group than alone, and a developed mind offers some benefits over ignorance as reflected in modern education's prioritisation of academic over vocational study. The status quo has advantages, which is why it is has so many members.

But are 'survival' and 'better grades' really reflective of improved living? Are they indicators that we are enjoying our precious time on earth to the full? I suggest that, no, they are not.

If you do what everyone else is doing, you will get what everyone else is getting. Our cognitive abilities allow us to choose to eschew the homogenous safety of the status quo. We can, instead, dare to go our own way. We can push our boundaries and blaze trails that may, or may not, scorch our fingertips, but either way we'll learn a great deal. We'll enjoy new vistas, meet new friends, discover new truths and feel the hum of life more intensely.

It won't always be a pleasure – not every new endeavour has positive outcomes – when we risk putting our head above the parapet we also risk being shot. But when we keep our head down amid our peers, we risk another death, that of the soul that sits confined to normalcy, wishing to reach for the heavens, but too afraid to leave the sanctity of what it knows.

Meaning and happiness

Over the years there has been much research into the upper tiers of Maslow's 'Hierarchy of Needs'; into happiness and what leads to it, in both the workplace and life in general. The findings are varied and interesting, but one conclusion is unquestionable – that people are happiest when they have a purpose – when their life has meaning.

What does it mean to have a life of meaning? This is an age-old question, the answers to which have filled – and continue to fill – many books. There is no single answer; meaning is as fluid as life itself, changing to fit time, circumstance, gender, race, culture and education. There is no one correct and universal response; life has whatever meaning you ascribe to it. By way of examples, for a parent, life's meaning may be found in raising a family; for a professional sports person, meaning may be found in a trophy. Both are equally valid.

In *Man's Search for Meaning,* one of the most profound books ever written, Holocaust survivor Viktor E. Frankl chronicles his experiences as an inmate in the Nazi concentration camps of the Second World War. He survived time in the Theresienstadt Ghetto, Auschwitz, Kaufering labour camp and the so-called 'rest camp' of Türkheim, and describes how those experiences led him to discover the importance of meaning in all forms of existence and after the war helped further shape his psychotherapeutic method, logotherapy.

Frankl says: 'There is nothing in the world, I venture to say, that would so effectively help one survive even the worst conditions as the knowledge that there is meaning in one's life.'

Away from the example of others, look at yourself; you might observe that when you are engaged in activities that are meaningful to you, life feels richer, fuller and probably happier.

In contrast, many surveys and reports find that workers across the globe are not happy. One finding, taken from a survey conducted by the UK human resources company, Investors in People, states that one in four employees currently feels unhappy at work. With so much of our time spent in the workplace, it's no exaggeration to call this torturous.

In the spirit of testing statistics for yourself, the Buddhist way, rather than accept these conclusions unquestioningly, ask around in your social circle. The high levels of work dissatisfaction among your friends and colleagues may surprise you.

So, if purpose and meaning equate to happiness, and evidence suggests that we are unhappy at work, it would be safe to conclude that for many, work isn't providing the necessary meaning. Which is probably why you are reading this book.

Of course, some people even when engaged in meaningful work are still unhappy. Meaningful workplaces are not a Utopia, and irritating work colleagues or demanding and abusive bosses may still exist in these environments. Yet those involved in meaningful work, about which they feel passionate, are often able to find the strength to persevere through these temporary challenges. Speaking from my personal experience as a writer: I enjoy the creativity of writing so much that I'm prepared to contend with the countless editorial 'rewrites' that might break the will of someone for whom writing is simply a pastime.

Simon, Chris and Dennis

In 2009, during the early days of 'TED talks', when they were little more than simple keynote presentations to small audiences, Simon Sinek took to the stage.

Without need for grand displays or props, Sinek stood in front of a simple whiteboard clutching an old-school microphone and delivered a talk that has been viewed over 40 million times on YouTube to date.

Sinek's talk was called 'Start with Why' and was an instant hit with fans of the TED format. And what he said was that we live our lives back to front. We live from a motivational framework of 'what' first, then 'how' and finally 'why'.

Sinek believes that we would be better served, and more successful, living our lives the other way around, ie. starting with *why* we do something, then moving on to *how* we do it and finally *what* we do. (His book, *Start with Why*, explains this idea wonderfully.)

Chris Anderson, 'Head of TED', in his book, *TED Talks: The Official TED Guide to Public Speaking*, echoes Sinek's idea.

Anderson, when advising others on the art of successful

public speaking, tells stories of TED presenters who have failed to keep the interest of their audience.

Unlike Sinek's meaning-filled presentation which attracted millions of online views, unsuccessful speakers have 'lost' their crowd by focusing too much on the minutiae of their presentation – the 'hows' and 'whats' rather than the meaning-driven 'why'.

Doctor of Philosophy Dennis Ford, in his book, *The Search for Meaning,* writes: 'Strategy – the _why_ or end questions – trumps the tactical _how_ and by _what_ means questions.'

My time as a tennis coach may allow me to add one last experience in support of Sinek, Anderson and Ford.

On the last day of my professional tennis coach's exam, taken in my early twenties, the examiner asked the students: 'What comes first, strategy or technique?' Each of us was expected to answer.

I was one of the last to be asked, and had heard almost all my peers say that it was essential for a tennis player to master the tricky techniques and skills of the sport first.

With my peer group offering opinions different from mine, I was tempted to join their chorus. When the examiner pointed at me, despite fearing public humiliation, I went with my gut feeling that: 'Strategy, in my opinion, should precede technique.'

The examiner raised an eyebrow, held my gaze for a moment and turned away. My heart sank and my friends stifled their laughter.

'Strategy, as Jardine says, should always precede technique,' he told the others. The explanation being that if you don't know where you want to hit the ball and why (hit low to a tall guy at the net so he has to bend his knees to reach it, for example), how can you choose the technique to use?

Life, it seems, is always better when we understand and know our 'why' – our reason for being or doing; our purpose and meaning in life. Yet finding our 'why' is not always as clear-cut as it seems. Worry not, the 'Buddhist Millionaire' philosophy is here to help.

Finding your 'wa'

Cheree Strydom and Sunni Jardine could not be more different. Cheree is a South African-born singer and songwriter in her late thirties and Sunni is an eighteen-year-old university student starting his career in professional rugby. What unites them, however, is their passion for what they regard as their 'jobs' – both of them epitomise the spirit of the 'Buddhist Millionaire' I described in the introduction.

Cheree comes from a musical family – her dad was a bass-guitar player – and she remembers, growing up sitting under the table listening to him perform. Her mother was insistent that her daughter should feel free to follow the music that was obviously 'in her blood'.

Her first professional performance was at the age of nine, and by eleven she was part of a touring band with other children, family and musician friends. Cheree had no difficulty in identifying her reason for being on this earth. She knew she was put on it to sing.

Unlike Cheree, many people don't know their calling with such certainty or from such a young age. I asked her what advice she would give to those who are not as assured of their place and meaning in life. She turned somewhat melancholy. 'I feel sorry for people who are stuck in a place where they haven't really found their purpose. My brother is an example; he's an accountant and he doesn't really enjoy it, yet my girlfriend is an accountant and loves what she does.

'I probably would say to them, you know what, maybe go and live a little. Maybe try and step out of your box a bit. Surprise yourself and do something completely unexpected. Something you wouldn't do normally. Go and challenge yourself a little bit in terms of doing something new... just dive into the unexpected, the unknown.'

Sage advice indeed.

One of the biggest challenges in life is to search for and find meaning – both existentially and personally. Our lives are better for a cause to champion, a reason to be and a path to tread knowing that it is taking us, one step at a time, to a destination that has value – for us at least.

But why is it so challenging to know who or what we want to be? Because most of us have either never been taught to search, or worse, were actively discouraged from doing so.

Cheree's earlier advice to novice searchers to 'step out of your box' is well meaning, but it misses a crucial ingredient: how to do so. An 'open mind' is a learned skill and like all skills must be nurtured, encouraged and practised to achieve mastery.

It was Cheree's parents who taught her to chase dreams. By encouraging her, imploring her even, to do what she loved, Cheree's mother taught her that doing what you love is the norm; her father did the same, by example.

However, many of us have not had parents like Cheree's, who actively promote the following of dreams and passions. Most of us have, instead, grown up in more didactic households with strict regimes and rules.

From the day that we are torn from a life of playing, to take our first steps into school, we are practising conformity, not dreaming or aspiring. We are living life by someone else's rules, and if our goals do not fit into the accepted norm, then they are frowned upon.

This is not an attack on parents and teachers; far from it. As a parent and teacher myself, I am all too aware of the difficulties and challenges of raising children. We all do the best we can with the skills, views and experiences we have to offer our charges at the time.

But, equally if we want to enjoy profitable work about which we are passionate, then we must take control of our lives and make the effort to search and find what is meaningful for us.

Like Cheree, my son, Sunni Jardine, knew from an early age what filled him with passion; it was rugby. However, his family weren't able to offer him the shared interest that Cheree's family could. Sunni said, 'I don't come from a background of high-level rugby, so that was something I kind of took for myself to go and do, from a young age, and something that I just fell in love with.'

Professional rugby encourages its stars of tomorrow to complete their academic education in preparation for a life beyond sport, the clubs providing a structure that allows youngsters to share their time between university demands and their professional rugby duties.

I asked 18-year-old Sunni what advice he would give other young people with families who, for whatever reason, may not necessarily share their child's academic or career aspirations, and this is what he told me:

'If you enjoy something, you just have to go and do it. You really do. You've got to take an individual role in that.

'As you get older and you start to mature, around fourteen, fifteen, I personally believe that's when you start taking a bit more control of your life. You can tell people what you like doing and you can start doing stuff by yourself.

'Parents are obviously going to have an influence on you but I think that's why it's down to you to just do what you want; not rebelliously – all due respect to parents – but you have to take control – and not let someone else make you do something you don't want to do.

'It doesn't have to be a confrontation; it can simply be an honest conversation.

'Just sit down and have a chat, and say, "Look, this is what I want to be doing. I would love for you to support me in doing that." You've got to act as an individual. Think for yourself.'

These are surprisingly wise words from someone so

young. My original reason for interviewing Sunni was to balance the spectrum of 'Buddhist Millionaire' voices. As our interview continued, though, I realised that Sunni had some excellent advice that would be relevant to all readers, whatever their age.

'As I said,' he continued, 'be a bit selfish. If the opportunity is there, and it's going to benefit you to do it, do it – and parents will always be there to support when you really need them.'

Putting yourself first

Choosing to go your own way, i.e. not living by other people's rules, requires us to put ourselves first – something that most of us find difficult to do. Buddhists do not share this hang-up about self-love being narcissistic or arrogant. At the heart of Buddhism is the practice of developing kindness and compassion for all beings, including ourselves.

Years ago, while dropping off my two young children at school one morning, I remember telling a fellow parent and friend of my decision to travel to Japan for the pilgrimage. He looked at me, horrified that I could leave my family to go on what he called a 'self-serving holiday'. Rather than perceiving my journey as a means of progressing mentally and spiritually for the sake of both me and my family (as was my intention), he saw a father failing to do his duty – i.e. sacrifice himself 24 hours a day, 365 days a year. For many, looking after number one is not seen as admirable, in Buddhism it is.

Buddhism's very logical and sensible teaching holds that if we cannot love ourselves enough to live a life that fills our hearts with passion, then what can we offer as motivation and example to those we want to inspire? It is the reason we are advised on a plane, in case of air pressure loss in the cabin, to put on our own mask before helping children and others in need. Not selfish. Practical.

Drew Sullivan is a man I look up to and another example of a Buddhist Millionaire. At over 6ft 6in tall he requires me to crane my neck back to look him in the eye. His physical size is matched by his undeniable presence.

Drew is like a walking Buddha: always smiling, gently spoken but ferocious and competitive enough to be one of the UK's best ever professional basketball players. Drew is also one of the humblest and giving men that I know. He makes a living doing what he loves and inspires fans with his exciting style of play.

Professional sport is not renowned for its egoless characters. Being centre stage to an adoring fan base is enough to corrupt many an athlete. Yet despite all his professional accolades (2012 Olympic Team GB Basketball captain, 3 x British Basketball most valuable player of the year, 2 x British League most valuable player of the year), Sullivan hasn't fallen into the narcissistic rabbit hole of sporting fame.

Such is Sullivan's gentle humility, that I only discovered

he played basketball by chance, after overhearing someone in our gym changing room talking about having seen him play on TV the previous weekend. When I asked Drew he simply smiled his massive smile and admitted, 'Yeah, I play a bit.'

Yet at the heart of this humble and giving man is the intuitive understanding that to look after others, you must first be able to look after yourself:

'[To some] this might sound like the most selfish thing in the world,' says Drew, turning serious, 'But your first responsibility with happiness is to yourself. You have no possible way of making anyone around you happy if you're not happy. If I go out of my way to make my wife happy, and I'm not happy, she knows it's not authentic, and it doesn't work.

'For a lot of people in a relationship, there tends to be the worry of taking care of their partner or their kids, but it can also lead to resentment if you don't follow your dreams.

'I hear people saying to their partners. The reason why I didn't follow my dreams is because I wanted to make sure you were okay first', says Drew shaking his head at the futility of this approach.

'Sometimes it's okay not to be okay. Not to go with the norm', says Drew with all the profundity of someone who, as a professional sporting star, has dared to live a life of which many merely dream.

'Wa' and 'Anti-wa'

Both Cheree and Sunni knew their passions early on. Let's investigate how to uncover yours, if it has not already revealed itself.

In Japanese, the word 'wa' means 'peace, harmony and balance'. You are going to use this word to guide you as you search for your meaning, or what Simon Sinek, author of *Start with Why*, calls your 'why'.

Think back to the question at the beginning of this book about having a million pounds (or any other large hypothetical figure suggesting that money is no longer your primary need). We have already established that you wouldn't return to your current job or workplace, so what would you do? What would you do with your time now that you no longer have the burden of making ends meet?

Many people at first give generic and superficial responses such as: 'I'd buy a car, a house and go on holiday.' These answers, while fine in themselves, lack honesty, creativity and, more importantly, meaning. We are not trying to uncover a rich person's shopping list; we are trying to find our deepest passions and reasons for being here on this earth.

As a pointer, let's keep the word 'wa' in mind. Our deepest passions, things that we truly love to do, always feel good to us. They feel harmonious, effortless, peaceful and joyful when we think of them. You'll know you are thinking about your deepest desires when you feel 'wa'.

In contrast, thoughts that make you feel tight, agitated, doubtful, fearful, heavy, guilty or a little nauseous, are 'anti-wa' feelings. For example, imagine a chore or meeting to which you have previously, grudgingly, committed even though you really didn't want to go.

So, let's begin – I recommend you take a pen and paper and set aside some quiet time for this.

Exercise 1: What if?

Think of things that you find inspiring and exciting that you would do with your new-found free time (now you are financially secure); things that you would only dream of doing; things that make you feel happy, joyful, peaceful and content; things that make you smile and feel grateful to be alive when you wake up in the morning. Think of things that would make you feel 'light' rather than 'heavy'; these are 'wa' things and point directly towards your 'why' for being alive. Write them down.

Let's keep uncovering and answer a second question: what would you do with your time if you had just six months (pain free) to live? Again, think in terms of the feeling of 'wa'; things that would make you feel happy and fulfilled. Write them down.

Let's add a final question: what would you do if you had a million pounds but only six months (pain-free) to live? You have all the money that you need but only a limited time to use it. Get writing.

Don't rush this process. Try to dig deep to search and uncover your purpose.

It's not uncommon, with this exercise, to come up with nothing on the first few attempts. We are not used to this type of creative, self-orientated work and your brain may initially resist the process. The resistance is normal. Creativity and soul searching take practice, but if you do the work, you will get answers.

When I do this exercise, I use the same process I use for writing books: I set myself a 25-minute time limit, pose the question and write down what immediately comes to mind, without filtering.

I then take a timed five-minute break, set the timer for a further 25 minutes and answer the second question. On completion, following another five-minute break, I spend 25 minutes writing my answers to the third question.

These initial answers form the first draft. Here are some examples of ideas from my first list:

Move to the Okavango Delta to write a novel; master the guitar solo to 'Sweet Child of Mine' (I am a child of the 70s after all) without making a single mistake; spend time with the Dalai Lama meditating.

I suggest that you repeat the process every day for a week until you end up with seven drafts.

As your brain works consciously and subconsciously on these questions throughout both day and night, it will reveal deeper and deeper answers, sometimes as flashes of personal insight or positive feelings.

At the end of the week, review your seven drafts and notice if any thoughts, ideas or words recur in all seven. Make a note of these.

Exercise 2: Standout moments

Now that you have written your seven drafts, it's time to make a note of ten key life experiences, standout memories or notable moments from your life so far.

By way of example, here are four of mine:

1. When my parents told me that my grandad Albert had died, I punched seven holes through my wardrobe door and sat sobbing in the back of the closet for hours.

2. The speech my karate sensei made about me as he presented me with my black belt moved me to tears. He honoured my hard work, dedication and fighting spirit.

3. Walking back to Ryozenji temple, both the start and finish point of the 88 Temple Pilgrimage, I knew not only that I had successfully completed the journey, but also that life would never be quite the same again.

4. Watching my son on television playing rugby for a professional team, I realised that I was living a vision that I had enjoyed during meditation many years before.

With your ten key life moments noted, look through them and identify any common themes and threads.

For example, browsing my four statements, you will notice a pattern of physicality (punching, karate, walking, rugby) but also one of existential searching.

Grandad Albert died when I was a child and it freaked me out. I worried a lot about death as a youngster and tried to fathom the point of existence if we were going to end up dying anyway.

Both karate and the Japanese pilgrimage were vehicles for self and spiritual understanding. I originally began karate, not to fight, but for the 'moving meditation' aspect of the sport – which I didn't find in the UK – searching instead further afield. Eventually this led me to Japan, walking the holy trail – the 88 Temple Pilgrimage. It was there that I learned that, essentially, we are the creators of our own destinies and I told my son: 'If you want to be a pro rugby player, go for it'.

Exercise 3: Seven layers of why

This is the last of the three exercises I am recommending for uncovering your life's purpose. Remember, if the answers engender feelings of 'wa', you are on the right track to finding your meaning. If they do not, keep searching until they do.

Think of something that you want and write it down. For example: I want a house by the beach.

This is a seven-step process, beginning with your desire.

1. **Question:** Why do you want a house by the beach?
    Answer: Because I want to walk my dog along the shore.
2. The answer to question 1 will become question 2.
    Question: Why do you want to walk your dog along the shore?
    Answer: Because I love to watch my dog run in and out of the sea.
3. **Question:** Why do you love to watch your dog run in and out of the sea?
    Answer:..
    ....
4. **Question:** Answer to question 3.
    Answer:..
    ....

5. **Question:** Answer to question 4.
    Answer:..
    ....
6. **Question:** Answer to question 5.
    Answer:..
    ....
7. **Question:** Answer to question 6.
    Answer:..
    ....

There you are; three excellent exercises to prompt you to dig and search for your 'why' in life.

If you are anything like me, you will be tempted just to read the words without doing the exercises, assuming that you'll do them in your head as you go about your day.

I urge you not to do this, because I can say, from personal experience, that these exercises work better if you give them full attention. And if my advice is not enough, why not take that of our eighteen-year-old rugby player: 'If the opportunity is there, and it's going to benefit you to do it, do it...'

As my mother used to say, 'Out of the mouth of babes...'

The 'F' word

By this stage, now that the curtains, hiding the illusion of money, have been drawn, you may have seen that money alone is unlikely to bring you contentment. Instead, you may be realising that a life of meaning, abounding with passion, is a more likely measure of happiness and fulfilment.

Yet despite this knowledge, some of you may still be floundering, stuck in your current job, and we should talk about why.

There is a phenomenon as unique to human consciousness as it is absurd: namely that, despite knowing the danger of and the damage caused by our limiting behaviours, we indulge in them nevertheless.

Why does a smoker still smoke despite knowing the harm that each drag of the cigarette undoubtedly causes him or her? Why does the heavy drinker still drink, while understanding that each sip is rotting the liver? Why do people stay in dysfunctional relationships even though they know instinctively that it won't be any better next week than it was this week or the last? And why do you remain in a job or career about which you are ambivalent at best?

The causes can be summarised by the 'F' words. In this context, F stands for Frills, Fear and Faith.

Let's look at each one in turn.

Frills

One of the key reasons we remain chained to harmful habits and unsatisfactory circumstances is that, at some level, it serves us to do so; the habits lead to some degree of pleasure. They give us, as a Cockney might say, a 'Frill'. (The Buddhists call this 'ignorance' – the idea that grasping at fleeting pleasure will lead to lasting happiness and enlightenment.)

As examples, let's take the smoker who still smokes despite witnessing a family member's demise from smoke-related lung disease, and also the abused partner who remains committed to a relationship despite being bullied. It's not unusual to hear the smoker protest that they enjoy the relaxation that comes with habitual smoking, or for the partner with the bruised self-esteem to admit that the 'ups' in the relationship by far outweigh the 'downs'.

Sometimes we are stuck simply because we enjoy being where we are.

And that is fair enough. If you are happy and content, stay where you are. There is no need to change and you may not want to.

Fear and Faith

However, there are others whose limiting habits and behaviours bring them no pleasure at all. These people genuinely want to change but are filled with *fear*, and their fear comes at the cost of its counterpart, *faith*.

Fear and faith, our two other 'F' words, are inextricably linked; an abundance of one often negating the other.

For example, if you had faith that all your wishes would be granted, would you have anything to fear? Probably not.

There is the counter-argument that in reality not all wishes are granted. All of us have experienced unfulfilled wishes, missed goals and broken dreams. Is it any wonder that the light of our faith fades?

But with a shift in perspective, there really is nothing to fear and every reason to have faith. When you make the effort to look from another angle, you will see that your failures, those things that you fear, are in fact not blockages to your success but stepping stones towards it. Faith appears when you trust that happiness and a fulfilled life come because of your failures, not in spite of them.

Let's use the example of a novice artist struggling to make a living from her work. From one perspective, with mounting bills to pay, it seems that every moment wasted on an inaccurate brushstroke is confirmation that it is simply too hard to make money doing what she loves; she falls into a downward spiral of despondency in the face of the hardship that comes with developing her craft.

From another angle, taking a slightly wider view, every incorrect brushstroke is actually a reference point towards one stroke that is correct. From this viewpoint there are no 'errors': she is either winning or learning. Faith in a positive creative process leads to a more relaxed frame of mind that inspires further creativity; an upward creative spiral that leads to mastery for which customers will, sooner or later, pay.

Before we are able fully to embrace this shift of viewpoint, it is vital to understand that both fear and faith are states of mind – choices we make about how we view the world – and it is up to us to direct our thoughts for our own advantage.

Playing to win – or not to lose

In life there are just two motivations: playing to win or playing not to lose.

Although on the surface both have the same end goal – to win the game – the motivating factors behind each are worlds apart.

The mindset of those playing to win is forward-thinking, positive, creative, courageous, charismatic, calm, powerful, hopeful and faithful. These types play for both the love of the game and winning the game; they are 'process' orientated.

In contrast, the mindset of those who play not to lose is

characterised by a passive attitude, doubt, stress, struggle and timidity. These types are often stilted and robotic in nature. They play out of fear of what is at stake should they lose; they are 'results' orientated.

Although both groups participating in the game ultimately want to win, their reasons for doing so are different. The winners are focused on the love of the game itself, which invariably leads to success, while those playing not to lose are focused on the defence of acclaim and the confirmation of status that comes with winning – or at least, not losing.

Dr Carol Dweck is a professor of Psychology and a leading researcher in the field of personality, social and developmental psychology. In her groundbreaking book, *Mindset*, she describes two types: 'growth mindset' and 'fixed mindset'.

From her research, she has concluded that growth-mindset people believe that their abilities, skills and futures are a work in progress, always fluid and never complete. Every experience is an opportunity to learn, grow and improve. Every failure is seen not as an indictment of worth, but a learning experience and a stepping stone to success.

In stark contrast, fixed-mindset people have a deep-seated belief that talent and ability are fixed traits and improvement is either limited or impossible: one is either fortunate enough to be born with a 'gift' ('I'm a natural linguist'; 'I've always been good at sports') or not. Because of their view that abilities are fixed and finite, they do not attempt to develop skills for which they consider they are not 'naturally inclined'. They also defend vehemently their 'talents' and often avoid situations where their talent can be questioned. Research shows that these people will choose easier challenges that confirm their skills, rather than harder challenges that might confirm gaps in their knowledge.

Let's look at examples of this. Imagine a child prodigy; a 'natural at maths' who enjoys the adoration of his or her marvelling parents and teachers. Such children delight in the power they wield over their peers, whom they leave for dust with their precocious genius.

These are children who have shown a level of mathematical ability above the norm. Because of their young age, their skills are viewed as natural gifts or 'God given'. They hear that they are 'lucky' and 'one in a million'. They have no control over their natural ability – they should be grateful that they were born as they were.

This belief in either you have talent, or you don't is fine until such talented children stand against fellow prodigies – an inevitable occurrence at some point in their lives.

Now they will be forced to defend their 'God-given' status. When they fail, which will happen from time to time when compared to others, or when faced with mathematical problems they cannot yet solve, they will believe that their failure indicates their arrival at the height of their 'fixed and natural gifts' and that they have nothing left to offer. Life is as good as over, at least as a 'maths genius'. In such cases, the child's ability has been undermined and belief in a fixed ability prevents further improvement to meet the new challenges. The child is left floundering.*

Let's look at another example from a totally different environment. In the sport of boxing, the most rare and coveted prize is the undefeated record. Two fighters wait nervously in opposing corners ready to do battle.

'Introducing first,' crows the boxing announcer, 'fighting out of the blue corner, wearing the multi-coloured trunks and weighing in at 139 pounds, a young man who captured Olympic gold in 1992 and now has a perfect professional record of 21 victories without a loss. Ladies and gentlemen, from east Los Angeles, California, Oscar De La Hoya.' The announcer takes time and pride in stressing to the crowd the facts of a 'perfect record'.

A boxer who enters the ring with an undefeated record begins the contest held in high esteem by the audience and with a mental advantage over his opponent. Countless

---

* Ironically, behind the scenes at home, such children are often raised being exposed to maths from birth, by parents motivated to provide a 'sound academic grounding'. By school age, when their 'natural talent' is identified, they will have been exposed to numbers (via various games, books, computer programs and the like) much more than their peers, many of whom are dealing with numbers for the first time. The real sources of the child's 'natural talent' are exposure and practice.

boxing tales tell fighters who were beaten by 'undefeated records' while still in the changing room, warming up and lacing gloves, long before a single punch had ever been thrown.

A no-loss record, however, also carries the burden of a 'fixed mindset'. Along with the intimidation and mental upper hand inherent in such a record comes also the pressure of defending it. There is never a shortage of young and hungry up-and-coming rivals shooting for the bull's eye, imagined on the champion's back.

An undefeated record, with all its attendant glory and rewards soon becomes a self-inflicted statement of a boxer's worth. The job of defending it becomes paramount, often at the cost of the passion once held for the art of pugilism; a passion that initially led the fighter to success.

The fighter no longer fights for the love of the game, but out of fear of maintaining a fickle and brittle illusion that one day must end. As the Buddhists, and Haraclitus, say, 'The only thing that is constant is change.'

Watching an athlete, team or individual play life not to lose rather than to win is uncomfortable. Who enjoys seeing a football team putting all their defenders on a line for 90 minutes to try to prevent a goal without themselves attempting to score at the opposite end of the field? Who would you prefer to pay to watch in the football World Cup, Brazil or Sweden?

There is something deeply unsatisfying about watching or being around those who, for whatever reason, are afraid of taking life by the scruff of the neck. It's why, instead, we prefer to attend inspirational talks, watch films with heroic protagonists and read uplifting books. We love to be inspired by people who are living their passion and telling others that it is not only possible, but also how to do it. Instinctively we know that we are designed to create, flourish, evolve and grow.

Fear keeps us chained to our limited lives, even though we know it is happening and that it is detrimental. Fear has many disguises but it always imprisons those suffering in its clutches. Whether it is the fear of losing something gained (an undefeated record), or fear of stepping into an uncertain future that we may or may not be equipped to handle, it never releases our best self: unless we change the way we view it.

How are our playing styles decided?

How then, did we become the style of player that we are? How and when did we decide to play the game of life defensively rather than proactively? How did we become a growth- or fixed-mindset type?

As with many of our behaviours, the answer is that they were gifted to us by our parents or primary carers and dominating environment. If you are a fearful and faithless adult, it's likely that this mindset was instilled in your upbringing.

When we are young with minds like sponges, but yet

without the skills of discernment, we absorb everything from our immediate environment without question. We are at the mercy of our elders; their beliefs, opinions, views, thoughts and fears.

Think about some of the thoughts and beliefs that hum in the background of your life, such as: 'Money doesn't grow on trees'; 'Look after the pennies and the pounds will take care of themselves'; 'Go to school and get a good education'; 'Very few people make it in professional sports so do something else just in case…'; 'I'm not good with numbers, maths is not my thing.' Are these ideas really yours? Can you remember a time when your direct experience formed these ideas? Probably not. It's likely that you inherited these beliefs. *Someone else's fear and opinion has become your habit.*

Let's meet up again with Selina Lamy, our Buddhist Millionaire and former Citibanker, whom we met in Chapter 2.

Years ago, when she returned, as a student, from a gap year spent travelling around Australia, Selina's parents decided that she 'needed to have a job when she got back'.

She worked for a while at a local veterinary practice, which she loved, but soon found herself applying for a corporate job position.

'When I look back, I should have been a vet,' says Selina. 'I can't remember how or why I made a decision to apply for a corporate job. *I thought everyone was doing it, so that was what I should do too…*'

Many people, like Selina, fall into lives carved out by others when they don't have the maturity to steer the course themselves. Though it's important to acknowledge the difficulty of the task ahead, it is never too late to regain control of our mental landscapes. If we wish, we can reshape our destinies with our own experiences accumulated as adults, freeing us from habits formed as children.

Changing beliefs, thoughts and habits is not easy, although it is entirely possible. You should be prepared to practise the new, better habits more than the old, so that they can be replaced. Just remember that you have practised being the 'old you', longer than the 'new you', so be patient and persistent. We'll look at how to do this in the third part of this book.

Fear is your friend; faith is its gift

Many of us have been taught that to retain our safety and security we must avoid the dangers that initiate fear. Ironically it is precisely danger and fear that are necessary to gain the security and safety that our guides covet for us!

By nature, we are purpose-driven creatures. If we are not moving forward then we are stagnating, then dying.

Take our hunter-gatherer ancestors as an example: without their desire and motivation to leave the cave for food we wouldn't be here today. They would have starved to death in their caves if they had succumbed to the fear of leaving it to hunt.

Thousands of years on, seven out of ten people are still sitting in their metaphorical caves; jobs that they don't particularly care for and are fearful of leaving in case the world outside eats them alive. Stagnation leads to death whether it be mental, physical, emotional or spiritual.

In April 2015, Archbishop Tutu and The Dalai Lama met in India to celebrate His Holiness's 80th birthday and to give a series of lectures and talks. The talks were on the subject of 'lasting happiness in a changing world'. Selected transcripts of the talks were published as *The Book of Joy*.

In the book, Archbishop Tutu talks about the work of a 'prenatal researcher' called Dr Pathik D. Wadhwa. 'It seems that science is confirming that stress and hardship are necessary for development in utero,' he writes, summing up some of the Wadhwa's findings.

'Our stem cells do not differentiate and become us if there is not enough biological stress to do so.

'If you want to be a good writer,' the archbishop continues, 'you are not going to become one by always going to the movies and eating bonbons. You have to sit down and write, which can be very frustrating, and yet without that you would not get that good result.'

The Buddhists summarise this idea in slightly more stark fashion with the first of their four noble truths: 'All life is suffering'.

This became clear to me, years ago, as an aspiring tennis pro when I twisted my ankle sliding to a ball on a clay tennis court in Florida.

I limped my way to the physiotherapist's room and learned something interesting. Except in the case of a serious break, you heal an ankle faster by immediately walking on it rather than using crutches and avoiding using the injured joint.

As long as the pain was not excruciating, the physio told me, by using the injured ankle, the flow of essential blood and nutrients would be encouraged and the joint would quickly heal itself to full repair. If, however, I continued to keep my weight off the ankle, blood and nutrients would be dispatched elsewhere, to other needy areas of the body. This would lead to chronic and recurring ankle injury, which I had seen with some of my tennis-playing peers.

The same thing happens in space. Because of the weightless environment, a human's bones lose mass because they no longer have to support themselves against gravity. There is no gravitational stress.

In contrast, on earth, gravity applies a constant mechanical load to the skeletal system. This causes healthy bones that maintain the density necessary to support the body. Action leads to growth and improvement. My old pathology teacher captured this idea in a nutshell with his much-loved phrase: 'Use it, or lose it!'

Moving on from examples of ankles and in utero

stem cells, what is it that we are losing by not overriding the stress and fears of uncertainty to pursue careers that we adore? What is it that we sacrifice when we settle for fulfilling other than our highest ideals or expressing our deepest passions? Our soul, that's what; the very essence of what it means to be human rather than an automaton.

The anatomy of fear

On different days two women faced the same attacker.

As one woman crossed the open playing fields after leaving the train station, a man approached her and asked her the time. Without hesitating, she pulled her sleeve to reveal her watch and give him the information.

The man snatched the watch, ripping it off her wrist, grabbed her throat and demanded that she hand over her bag too. Frozen with fear, she could do nothing, and he took her bag and watch and ran away.

On another day the same attacker, in the same place, attempted to distract another woman with the same question. But this time as he reached for her watch, she grabbed his hair with her free hand and hurled obscenities at him while slapping and kicking him.

On hearing the noise, passers-by rushed to help. At that point, it was the attacker who was more in need of assistance than the woman.

These two examples are not about self-defence strategies. They are about fear and how it can manifest so differently in people experiencing the same scenario.

Fear is a word that we use to describe the uncomfortable physical feelings we have when facing either a genuine or perceived threat. The physical feeling: butterflies in the stomach, narrowing of vision, sweaty palms, weakness in the legs and shortness of breath are just some of the symptoms of two powerful hormones in the body secreted in preparation for danger. These hormones are cortisol and adrenalin. The hormones are essentially a human super-fuel. They prime and prepare the body to be magnificent in the face of adversity so that we may survive and thrive to see another day.

Both women would have had bodies full of cortisol and adrenalin when facing their assailant, but why did one woman freeze and the other become super-charged? Once again, to quote my old pathology teacher: 'Use it or lose it.'

With the body charged and raring to go, the hormonal super-fuel must be 'released' in order to be beneficial. Think of a frightened antelope outrunning a lion – it has put its foot on the metaphorical accelerator and is using every drop of adrenalin and cortisol to outrun those claws and teeth at its flank. In this scenario the acronym FEAR could stand for: Feeling Energised And Ready.

On the other hand, for every second this super-fuel stays unutilised within our bloodstream, it becomes a heavy and sinking burden – like gold on a stream bed – and we freeze, inactive.

Run or fight: if we don't use the adrenalin, we lose its benefits. For Ever A Rabbit (frozen motionless in the headlights of a car), would be a suitable acronym for FEAR in this example.

If we fail to engage in life's battles, the internal strength that we have been afforded both to survive and thrive lies dormant. If we don't use it, we lose its benefits. We must act.

If we are to aim for a life of work that is both rich and meaningful then we must be brave. We must understand that fear and stress are our friends. They are a cocktail of super hormones designed to fuel our success, not indicators of cowardice. We must activate the adrenalin and cortisol, heart and soul, mind and body and take early and immediate steps of action as soon as we feel the butterflies and jitters in our tummies.

The late great Nelson Mandela said this of fear: 'I learned that courage was not the absence of fear, but the triumph over it. The brave man is not he who does not feel afraid, but he who conquers that fear.'

Motivations to action: tragedy, desperation and choice

Sometimes we are forced to face our fears; backed into a corner where the only way out is to find our best self, as Selina Lamy explains: 'My work has always been up and down, but it had gone down and there was no up. I was getting nothing out of it; I just knew I had to change something. I couldn't do it any more. I was miserable, and I was coming home grumpy and exhausted.

'Then the world turned on its head. My brother who I knew had been suffering with cancer, went very rapidly downhill. I was with him every weekend, and it [the cancer] had gone to his brain. He'd lost his mobility and his mind and on the third of November, he died.'

'After Jason passed away, I felt that his life was far too short, and I know there were things he wanted to do that he will now never do. And then I thought that it's not good enough to be a slave to the corporate dollar. It's really not enough. Life is too short. I owe it to my brother to chase a wonderful life because he can't any more.'

There is a Buddhist story that also focuses on death's potential as a catalyst for meaningful change. It tells of a woman whose young child lies dead in her arms.

Distraught and frantic, she carries the child around her village asking for help.

Seeing death in the child's face, the villagers are sad to tell the mother that they are unable to assist. One, however, suggests that she visit the Buddha.

Laying the child at the Buddha's feet, the mother begs him to bring her child back to life.

The Buddha tells the woman that in order to heal her child and her sadness she has to go back to her village and bring back a mustard seed from every home that has never known death.

With tears streaming down her face, she knocks on door after door only to hear: 'I'm so sorry, we cannot give you a mustard seed, death has visited this family before.'

Back at the Buddha's feet, now holding her dead son in her arms one last time, she finally understands the Buddha's lesson of the inevitability of death.

One hears this type of story time and again – tragedy serving as a catalyst for change – whether it be in a religious text or a personal story. Just as Mandela, Archbishop Tutu and Pathik Wadhwa, the prenatal researcher, attest: stress is sometimes necessary for change.

Yet tragedy is not necessary in order to motivate change; a simple choice is enough to do the trick. But I can almost guarantee that, as you reach outside of your comfort zones, you will experience a stress, pain and doubt over money.

In these challenging times, it may help to keep in mind this passage by W. H. Murray from his 1951 book, *The Scottish Himalayan Expedition*:

Until one is committed there is hesitancy, the chance to draw back, always ineffectiveness. Concerning all acts of initiative (and creation), there is one elementary truth, the ignorance of which kills countless ideas and splendid plans; that the moment one definitely commits oneself, then Providence moves too... A whole stream of events issues from the decision, raising in one's favour all manner of unforeseen incidents and meetings and material assistance which no man could have dreamt would have come his way.

For Murray, his faith in 'Providence' was enough to lead him through fear and doubt. I have wondered, then and now, what is the 'Providence' that moves in order to support the brave?

Naturally, our three traditional pillars of thought all have their opinions: religion may call it God, science may prefer the theory of the 'evolution of natural selection' and philosophy may choose to toe a middle line, somewhere between the two.

Honestly, I cannot confirm what force, mechanical or divine, is at play when manifesting the wishes of the brave. I wish I knew, but I don't; I can only say that something works in our favour when we ignite ourselves with the flames of passion and meaning.

At first, your initiating action may be to trust that what I say is true, until you have experienced success enough times for you to believe wholeheartedly and for your faith to blossom.

But what is the alternative? That you stay stuck where you are forever more, peering over the fence at the life you dream you could live? Trust me. Scale the fence. All will be well. I'll see you on the other side where some important information is waiting that will make the process easier.

Part III

The Path of the Buddhist Millionaire

The path between
money and meaning

Congratulations. You chose to scale the fence to the other side. Already, you and I have come quite a way together and I'm grateful for your companionship. We started this journey on the path of money – it's a road most walk without realising that there are alternatives. Having accepted that the way of money might not lead us to the level of satisfaction previously assumed, we took the path of meaning in search of deeper purpose for our lives.

Yet despite the knowledge that there is more to life than money, it cannot be denied that a life of meaning alone is not enough. Those brown envelopes containing bills will still land on our doormats, regardless of our purpose-driven lives; the banks will continue to demand their fees, irrespective of our values.

In Part III, we will continue our journey together on a middle way, weaving between the extremes of financial success and deeper motivations. It will be a way respecting the realities of living in a modern material world, with all its demands, while simultaneously honouring deep-seated passions and purpose. It is the way of the Buddhist Millionaire.

But first, we need to prepare ourselves with a little more knowledge.

There are nine lessons that provide the backbone of the Buddhist Millionaire's way, as revealed to me when I walked the 88 Temple Pilgrimage.

As stated in the introduction to this book, although the lessons were learned while on a Buddhist trail, it is not necessary to be Buddhist to enjoy them – just human. They are equally as applicable to any race, colour, creed, gender or religious denomination.

But before I explain the nine lessons, I'd like to say a few words about the path itself.

In Japanese, the word for path is *dō* (pronounced 'doh', but without the Homer Simpson accent). The kanji (the calligraphic pictogram) for the word *dō*, like so many in written Japanese, can have myriad meanings. Only two concern us here.

The first meaning is somewhat mundane and translates as 'road'– literally the earthly gravel and ground of a road or pathway.

The second has a more spiritual connotation and translates as 'way' – a path that guides the journey of life.

To walk a path in the spirit of *dō* is to do more than use the path as a means of getting from A to B. To walk a *dō* is to embrace and commit wholeheartedly to both the path and its final destination. Thus the *dō* becomes a way of life, rather than a shortcut to a goal; it is both the means and the end.

You might recognise *dō* in some of the Japanese words that have become part of our own lexicon: judo: the Japanese martial art of throwing an opponent; aikido: another martial art, but one notable for its turning movements where opponents are thrown to the ground seemingly with little effort; shodo: the beautiful Japanese art of brush calligraphy; kendo: the art of bamboo sword fighting; zendo: a Japanese meditation hall.

To journey on a *dō* path is art, with all the nuance, subtle balance and unpredictability that art entails. As such, *dō* connects us to that 'bigness' touching all artists; that source of all things from which we emanate.

Just as the brushstrokes of the Japanese calligrapher (shodo) swirl and swoop, and the arms and bodies of the martial artist (aikido) twist and turn, so too will your journey on the path we are embarking on.

Take your time. Enjoy every step. Smell the flowers along the way and reap the rewards at the end.

The art of pilgrimage

To walk a pilgrimage is *dō*. People have walked pilgrimages for thousands of years: the 88 Temple Pilgrimage in Japan, Lourdes in France, the Camino de Santiago in Spain, the Pilgrim's Way in England, the Abraham Path in the Middle East, to name just a few.

Committing effort to travel, often hundreds of miles, to sacred sites and shrines is one of the most powerful and effective spiritual practices available for anyone searching for answers to the confounding questions of life.

Walking is as old as humankind. Initially walking from point A to point B was from necessity, a mode of human transport, but anyone who has ever trekked, hiked or orienteered will testify that walking has many more benefits than mere locomotion.

John Muir (1838–1924) is one of America's most famous and influential conservationists, and an environmental trailblazer. In California particularly, he is an icon and often referred to as 'The Wilderness Prophet.'

Muir's words and actions helped inspire President Theodore Roosevelt's innovative conservation programmes, including the establishment of seventeen national monuments such as the world-famous Grand Canyon and Muir's namesake, Muir Woods.

Muir was renowned for his exciting adventures in California's Sierra Nevada and Alaska's glaciers.

'Thousands of tired, nerve-shaken, over-civilized people are beginning to find out that going to the mountains is going home. Wilderness is a necessity,' said Muir of the value of getting out, presumably on foot, into nature.

One hundred years on and closer to home (London), Ian McClelland has picked up the flame of wilderness travel and is lighting the lives of those who walk alongside him.

Ian is an interesting man; full of life and passion and a skilful opponent on the mats of Brazilian jiu jitsu (a wrestling- and grappling-based martial art), which is where I first met him.

Like all people of character, forged through direct, honest and hard-earned experience, he is quick to downplay his achievements and slow to beat his own drum; he skipped very quickly over his bachelor's degree in Healthcare. Ian is a man of action. He walks the walk – literally.

Ian leads small groups of people on expeditions to some of the most awe-inspiring natural destinations across the globe, including Nepal, Iceland and Finland. His interest doesn't lie in the goal-driven sport of mountaineering, but in the life- and soul-changing experience of pilgrimage, and communing with nature in its most undiluted state.

'Anyone can walk,' says Ian; 'it's within the realms of everybody.

'When we are walking there in the mountains, we don't have the constant drone of mobile phones, TV, the internet, adverts telling you what you should and shouldn't wear.

'Instead we are instilling the mountains into them [the walkers], and their thermostat of reality changes.'

Ian is one of the many examples of people in this book who spend their time doing what they love and making a living as he does so. He is a prime example of a man who has found the balance between money and meaning, not least because his passion also benefits others.

There are deep benefits to be gained from the extended silence and solitude that both pilgrimage and communing with nature afford.

Imagine a closed jar filled with water and with some mud at the bottom. If you picked up the jar and shook it, you would have a muddy version of a child's Christmas snow globe. This is a symbol for our mind, which we will explore in more detail later.

Before pilgrimage, during the humdrum of daily living, we may not even notice the chaos in our metaphorical muddy jars. We are often too busy whizzing about our days.

During the earliest stages of pilgrimage (for me it was within the first fourteen days), there is enough silence to notice that there is a jar.

With continued silence and undistracted living, we become curious about the contents of that jar – all the mud twisting and turning this way and that within the water. We hadn't previously noticed that our thoughts were so disparate and fractured.

With further silence and simple living, we might notice that our swirling thoughts are, at last, beginning to subside, just as the mud settles at the bottom of the jar when it is no longer agitated. We are no longer adding to the turmoil by overthinking things, and stop checking our social media status or fretting about news bulletins.

Much later, as more and more muddy thoughts settle,

the water becomes clearer and begins to reflect a sense of the calm reliable power that was always there in us, but was just obscured by cloudy thinking.

This is our deepest self – our soul, our Buddha nature, our inner flame, God, our happy place. The names don't matter, because when we open to this 'self', we'll recognise the essence; it will feel less like a discovery and more like reuniting with an old friend who has always been there, if just somewhat out of sight. This is the same essence we feel when we look up at the sky, out to sea or into a flame.

This is the source of serendipity and providence that W. H. Murray (whom we referred to in chapter six) talks of in his book, and which Ian uses to help 'reboot his teams of walkers'; it is the source of your personal power, the power which you will come to trust to help you live the life and do the work of your dreams.

When walking the path of the Buddhist Millionaire, we will be reuniting with this personal power and also utilising the following nine key lessons revealed to me during my pilgrimage in Japan.

I have used these same lessons, alongside regularly reconnecting to my personal power, to architect my own life successfully, and I offer them here for you to do the same if you wish.

The lessons are:

1. Start from where you are
2. The art of 'one-stepping'

3. When the student is ready – hey presto – the teacher appears
4. The art of effortlessness
5. Recharging the batteries
6. Small wins
7. The law of karma
8. Love and gratitude
9. Coming full circle – you knew it all along

I will be outlining these in more detail in the next part of the book. You should now be clear about where you want to go. The 'finding your wa' exercises will hopefully have helped you determine the purpose and passion that is going to be your new 'work'. If you're still deliberating, don't worry. This is a constantly evolving process and even the most decisive readers may well have to change their route as they go along.

Lesson 1:
Start from where you are

'I am what I am.'

– Shirley Bassey

It is said that a 'journey of a thousand miles begins with a single step', but this maxim is incomplete; there are steps before that all-important moment.

Before any step can be taken, we must first decide where we want to go – in this case, it is towards meaningful, profitable work. It is also essential to recognise and accept the starting point of our adventure. Then, and only then, are we suitably equipped to begin.

Many years ago, when I was setting up my first business – a shiatsu clinic just outside of London – I took some advice from the husband of my Japanese-language teacher. Eiko is a wonderfully elegant Japanese lady who steered me to success in my language exams and introduced me to her husband, Jim, whom I treated for back pain. Shiatsu is a manual body therapy of Japanese origin. It is a hybrid of stretching, massage, physiotherapy and osteopathy played out against a backdrop of traditional far-Eastern medical theory – meridians, pressure points, chakras etc. Shiatsu is essentially acupuncture without the needles.

During the time Jim was a patient, my shiatsu practice was a 'mobile clinic'. With a futon strapped to my back, I visited houses in and around London, fixing backs, sorting knees, easing migraines, calming minds and dishing out advice on healthy living. I loved it. Eventually the time came to expand my horizons and find a permanent site for me to offer my treatments from, and it was Jim who was instrumental in my success – but not in a way that I enjoyed.

Nearing his mid-sixties, Jim had created, developed and then sold several very successful businesses – all had been sold for six- or seven-figure sums. Large companies recruited him as a consultant and troubleshooter. Jim offered me advice purely, I think, because he enjoyed watching people trying to take charge of their work and business lives and push their financial evolution; but he was as brutal as he was benevolent.

One week, after completing his shiatsu treatment, Jim asked me how my new clinic was going. I told him that it was going great, doing well and coming along nicely. He allowed this generic answer just once.

The next time he asked about my new clinic and I

offered a vacuous non-committal summary of its health, he looked me straight in the eyes and sent me to his desk to retrieve a pen and sheet of paper:

'Matt,' said Jim, without taking his eyes off me, 'how is the business going?' He then ordered me to write down on the paper the number of clients I had treated at the clinic in the past week. I wrote down three, and couldn't look him in the eye.

The truth was that my 'grand business move', my upscale from roving shiatsu therapist to serious business contender with my own clinic, was not taking off quite as I had expected. Jim knew it. I knew it too, but was too ashamed to admit it to him, and more importantly, to myself.

'Writing down the facts is not about judging yourself,' Jim taught me, 'but how can you expect to succeed if you cannot honestly and openly admit what needs fixing? Writing it down makes it concrete – undeniable. Once you know where you are, you know what you need to work out to get to where you want to go.'

It was a business and life lesson that has stayed with me ever since and brought me many rewards. Wherever we find ourselves in life is right and appropriate. We are who we are at any given point in time and it is impossible to be anything else. If we could have done better, we would have done better. If we could be in a better position in life, we would be in a better position in life. Worry or denial will not change the facts.

Stepping off the plane after arriving in Japan at 2am on a cold February morning, I stood outside the locked gates of Ryozenji temple, the first of the 88 temples constituting the famous pilgrimage.

As I stood there, freezing, I realised that I knew next to nothing of the detail of the journey ahead. I had made the decision to walk the Pilgrimage virtually overnight, on an inspired whim and without doing any meaningful research. Following Jim's advice and now faced with a situation where denial would have been futile, I took an honest inventory of my plight. I admitted to myself that I knew literally nothing of the task ahead. I was about to step, as good as blind, onto a path about which I knew nothing, but wanted to tackle regardless.

This self-admission of my overwhelming ignorance at least allowed me to steel myself, 'bite down on my gumshield', as they say of boxers in an unwinnable fight, and prepare for the arduous journey of self-discovery that was to come.

Just as I once tried to bluff Jim about my business, few of us are prepared to be honest with ourselves and others about where we currently stand in life. It's as if we are frightened to be honest about our 'status' in case it doesn't match up to others' arbitrary expectations and confirms our lack of success. I suspect that, by burying our heads in the sand, we are attempting to avoid the painful truth that we are not yet where we want to be or who we want to be. Instead, we ignore where we are, inflate our success when retelling stories and post only our best photos and status on social media sites.

Yet, this denial of circumstance does nothing to improve our situation; all it does is gain a plethora of empty 'likes' for a Facebook post. When we deny where we stand we also deny ourselves access to the critical thinking skills, motivation, energy and providence that are mobilised to allow us to move from where we are to where we want to be.

The first step in creating a work life about which you are utterly passionate might simply be to admit that you are currently not where you want to be. And that's okay. It's a great honest beginning, from where the only way is up.

You might find the following exercise helpful. Fill the gaps in these sentences:

I, *[your name:]* _____, am currently making my living *[your current work:]* _____ _____, and I find it *[your feelings about it:]* _____ _____; if I'm honest, what I would really like to do is *[write where you want to be and what you want to do:]* _____ _____.

Here's a mock example if you are stuck:

I, _Fred Flintstone_, am currently making my living _making square pegs for round holes_, and I find it _really boring and tiring_; if I'm honest, what I would really like to do is _write a book about dinosaur welfare_.

Acceptance, self-esteem and the Western tragedy

Dukkha is a Sanskrit* word, used in Buddhism, that roughly translates as 'unsatisfactoriness'. Buddhists use it to describe the stress, anxiety and suffering that occur without fail, many times, during the course of our lives. Dukkha encapsulates the stress that comes from trying to change or manipulate things that cannot be controlled – fitting square pegs into round holes, so to speak. This, for most of us, is the crux of our daily dissatisfaction – the deep-rooted source of the Everywhere Nowhere of which we spoke in Part I.

The concept of dukkha can be seen in many places. Keeping up Appearances was a British television sit-com in the 1990s and an entertainment staple for many Brits now in their forties. The programme followed the misfortunes of a working-class woman, Hyacinth Bucket, ('Bouquet', as Hyacinth would correct those who dared pronounce her surname like the vessel for carrying water), as she struggled to gain standing with the upper echelons

---

* Sanskrit is the ancient language of Buddhism.

of society. As a parody, it is hilarious because, to some extent, we can all recognise in ourselves a little bit of Hyacinth's need to 'keep up with the Joneses'.

Our minds are beautiful things; human consciousness is a wonderful gift that separates us from the rest of the animal kingdom. But this elixir of critical thinking can also be a poison. When in balance, our cognitive faculties allow us to create, evolve, dream and both set and achieve goals. However, out of balance, they can blight us with stress, fear, self-doubt and dissatisfaction – and set us on a downward slope to deep discontent.

Modern society and economies encourage us towards discontent and lure us into endless striving; if we are not 'growing' or 'keeping up with the Joneses' then we are failing and falling behind. This is the hidden psychology waged against us by businesses with sales strategies urging us to 'upgrade'. FOMO – the Fear of Missing Out – is another marketing tactic that is used against us, for example in adverts or promotions that suggest that 'stocks are limited' or that 'this offer will end in three days'.

The unspoken intimation is that if we miss out on the 'latest upgrade model' or 'the new super-duper gadget' we are in some way lacking or inferior. Most of us have experienced being caught in this consumer web, waiting helplessly for its weaver to feed us with the next empty offering. In this way we are not much better off than an addict waiting for the next fix.

When this happens, we have unquestioningly fallen

into dukkha. We are resisting, denying even, where we are and instead buying 'stuff' to create the illusion that we are somewhere better.

The antidote to dukkha is self-acceptance and its counterpart is contentment, but they are both arts that must be cultivated. It takes practice, skill and effort to resist the temptation to self-flagellate for every minor indiscretion, fault or frailty in our make-up. Paradoxically, without self-acceptance and contentment, it is next to impossible to set, reach for and attain goals. We must learn to balance accepting where we are in life with where we want to go without condemning ourselves for not yet arriving. This paradox plagued me for many years until its resolution during the 88 Temple Pilgrimage.

One of the key teachings of Buddhism is that it is our striving (what Buddhists often call 'grasping') that leads to discontent and unhappiness. We are either ruminating over the past or fretting over the future, thereby missing the gift of the only time there can ever be – the present.

For a long time, I feared that following a life of acceptance and contentment – the Buddhist way – would mean having to abandon all goals, and I'd be destined instead to veg out in a sort of somnambulant hippie fog devoid of all ambition. I love setting goals and achieving them; it makes me feel alive. I think striving and evolving honours the wonder of life. I'm certain Charles Darwin would have agreed.

Yet during the 88, I learned that self-acceptance and

contentment don't exclude us from attempting to better our position in life; they free us up to do so more easily.

It was an insight that came to me roughly halfway around the pilgrimage trail. I had sat down at the foot of the steps of one of the temples I had visited, taken my rucksack off my back, and was tucking into one of the big juicy oranges (*mikan*) that grow abundantly on Shikoku. It hit me, as insights often do, out of the blue: Buddhists have walked the 88 Temple Pilgrimage in search of enlightenment for hundreds of years, and was enlightenment not also a goal? Was this not a form of discontent and grasping? Surely a contented monk, self-accepting of his position in life, would simply stay in the temple and meditate.

Then I realised that the lesson about grasping was not about non-achieving; this would be impossible. Since the first cell divided into two, we have been striving and reaching for another, maybe a better, tomorrow. It is part of the natural order. The Buddhist lesson on grasping, then, is not encouraging ambitionless inertia, but self-creation and reinvention, just without the stress, guilt and doubt to which we have become accustomed. In this way, we are playing for the love of the game rather than fearing the loss. And it feels good. Actually magnificent. This is the source of the joyful butterflies we feel when we leap out of bed in the morning for a work life that we totally cherish. Filled with love and passion for what we do, there is no room for the negative, only the positive and success has a funny way of following the joyful.

Winner of MasterChef

One of my favourite aspects of writing this book was interviewing the many people who, knowingly or not, are successfully walking the path of the Buddhist Millionaire. Another of these is Druhv Baker.

In 2010, Mexican-born, Indian-raised Dhruv Baker left his job in media sales to take part in the 2010 series of the hit BBC programme, MasterChef. He won with some stunning, delicious and passion-infused culinary creations. Dhruv is a perfect example of a Buddhist Millionaire and he had some valuable insights about others in his industry who are equally fulfilled and successful:

'They're all insanely passionate, they've always got a smile on their face, they are immensely successful in the terms that traditionally we view success, which is invariably financial return,' Druhv told me. 'But actually, the money is a secondary thing. Some of them have got more money than I can even imagine. They still work because they love what they do.'

Traditional financial markers of success are what many of us strive to achieve in order to keep up with the Joneses, often at the expense of our happiness. I wondered, along with Druhv, if the markers could be different.

'There's a scale,' said Druhv; 'at one end we've got the

traditional marker of success – money – and on the other end of the scale, someone like my supplier in France, an old Frenchman, who's madder than anyone I know. He has a two-acre plot where he grows these extraordinary products with flavour like nothing you've ever had before.

'This old Frenchman works for around eight months a year. His life doesn't change at all. After he's worked his eight months, he just sits around and drinks coffee and smokes cigarettes and he's perfectly happy. You could say "here's ten million quid to upscale your production" and he'd look at you like you were insane.

'He's deeply content... It's not that he has settled, or given up striving. I think that does him a disservice. He's content and he's happy.

'For these types of people, the financial side of life is irrelevant. I think sometimes people have to have the financial side to compensate for the fact that they've got an empty life,' concluded Dhruv.

His story helps to highlight one of the key points of this chapter: happiness is not exclusive to the contented, just as success is not exclusive to the goal-driven. It is possible, and acceptable, to be either or both. If you wish to strive and make money – no problem; if you wish to work a few months of the year and while away the rest sipping coffee – why not? The common denominator, however, is a life lived with passion rather than fear, and being content with and honest about the decisions that you make, lofty or otherwise.

Now that you've honestly assessed the starting point of your journey, and looked ahead to where it might end, it's time to work out how to tackle such a mammoth task.

Lesson 2:
The art of one-stepping

'How do you eat a mammoth? One mouthful at a time!'

– Proverb

'Nants ingonyama bagithi Baba Sithi uhm ingonyama…'

–Lebo M, 'The Circle of Life'

The Zulu words at the beginning of the song from *The Lion King*, 'The Circle of Life', send a tingle up the spine and signal the beginning of a procession of animals that walk, meander, skip and dance down the theatre aisles, almost brushing elbows with stunned and captivated theatre-goers. For the next two and half hours, the audience will be transfixed by the sensuous colours and glorious sounds of the hit musical and become lost in the make-believe of the entertainment.

I was in the audience with my wife to watch George Asprey play the villainous lion of the show, Scar. It's a role he's played for over ten years, an uncommonly long time for West End theatre runs that usually last no more than six months. I was fascinated to learn from George how he managed to keep his role so vibrant, passionate and believable after all this time.

'I have never not looked forward to going into work,' George told me afterwards. 'Of course there are days when your voice isn't good; it's like at the moment, my voice isn't too good, and I've got a bunion on my foot; it's a bit painful, and you know the show's going to be difficult, but I never have that feeling of "I really don't want to go to work today".'

It's the primary skill of an artful actor or actress: to give so much of themselves that the audience get lost in their performance.

'I think you can take it for granted as an actor, the way you make an audience member feel,' says George. 'But so many times when I'm going home on the train, and I'm sat in the carriage with a family who's just been to see the show, and all they're doing is enthusing and the kids are buzzing.'

'Theatre gives so much more than just the two and hour half hours of the production. It's a live piece, it's totally immersive and when the audience are on fire and they're laughing at everything and getting every joke, it just fills your heart with complete ebullience; you go on stage with confidence and love and respect for the audience and everything. The relationship is symbiotic.

'So when you feel you can affect someone through your performance, when you see someone affected by what you've done and you hear people saying, "I was absolutely in tears at the end", that's because of what you've done. You've affected emotion in another human being. If you're in a relationship you can do that. In a way, we are in a relationship with the audience.'

The way he talks about his work feels almost prophetic, and when I asked George about it he replied: 'I'm slightly hesitant to use the word religious, but I think there's something spiritual about it.'

George's passion for his art and subsequent success clearly qualifies him as a Buddhist Millionaire, but it was something else that drew me to interview him.

Acting is one of those creative careers, alongside singing, professional sports, writing and art, which is notorious for being almost impossible to break into and many dream of but few ever realise.

In the face of the mammoth task as 'making it in show business', many either give up their dreams entirely and settle for careers that simply pay the bills, or lower their expectations and settle for much less than they once desired. Except George. And I wanted to know his secret.

Just like many others, George was drawn to acting from an early age: 'Ever since I was a little kid, I was always doing school plays, impressions of people and was always the class clown in a way. I think I knew what I was going to do from the age of three.'

He went on to explain his route from A to B following his school days:

- At nineteen, after a brief spell in the army, George moved to America to attend business school.
- While in the US, in his free time from business studies and for fun, he took another course: Acting 101.
- After taking part in an Acting 101 cottage play, he was approached by a woman who recommended he return to London to attend LAMDA (London Academy of Music and Dramatic Art) with a view to pursuing a career in acting.
- In 1990, George graduated from LAMDA and secured his first professional acting job in pantomime, playing the front end of "Maggie the Cow".
- After finally receiving his Equity card, George spent the next four years playing various parts in musical theatre productions such as *Guys and Dolls*, *The Sound of Music* and *Scrooge*.
- George was then awarded a small film part in Kenneth Branagh's *Frankenstein*.
- After *Frankenstein*, he was offered his first lead role in a film (*The Dying of the Light*), for which he was nominated for a BAFTA award.
- He went on to work for a number of years on the

'TV circuit' in various productions, before getting another lead in a film – *The Greatest Game Ever Played* – about golf.

- In 2006, George returned to the musical theatre stage to play the part of 'Billy Flynn' in the musical *Chicago*.

- It was after *Chicago* that George won the part of Scar in *The Lion King*.

When you consider George's 'path to stardom', it is evident that it has been a long, hard road to his well-earned success. He wasn't a precocious child prodigy destined for immediate stardom. George has studied, worked (often in mediocre parts), learned, worked and studied again until he finally reaped the rewards of his years of service to acting. There has been, as you can see, no short cut.

When learning about the realities of other people's successful journeys, it is easy to be overwhelmed by the amount of time, blood, sweat and tears that were entailed to scale a difficult career ladder. At the same time we have a tendency to listen to, and take note of, only the exciting parts of any given story: the beginning and the end. And yet, it is in the 'tiresome middle' where success is made, and this is the reason I have spent time in this book attempting to help you uncover your life's passions.

Life has its hard times, and when we are enjoying the road we have chosen to walk, it is easier to survive the journey when troublesome times undoubtedly arise. By contrast, if our choices are merely based on the latest fad or pastime, it will be near impossible to muster the motivation to get us over even the smallest humps along the way.

The long middling miles, bookended by inspired starts and celebratory ends, are where we will spend the majority of our time while on this journey. On the 88 Temple Pilgrimage, a microcosmic representation of life, Temple 1 represents birth, Temple 88, death; the rest are the years between. Anyone who has been witness to the magical early days after the birth of their child can attest to them quickly giving way to the arduous years of routine once back home from hospital.

Yet this admission of the reality of the 'tiresome middle' doesn't besmirch life; rather, I would argue, it confirms its majesty. Once the initial excitement of a love affair is over, in its place, aside from the snoring, clothes left on the floor and toothpaste lids left off tubes, is hopefully a deep, rich, mature and wonderfully 'ordinary' love that is as wonderful as it is routine. This depth is a rare commodity in the modern click, buzz and swipe world that extols the empty virtues of immediate gratification.

The truth is, life is hard work. Thankfully. Nothing meaningful ever came without elbow grease. That's isn't to say that life is a depressing slog; not at all. It is to say that life has wonderful lessons that can only be appreciated if you've committed to the game long enough to learn them.

As I walked the 1,400 km between Temple 1 and 88, I realised something that George must have realised in his many years since starting out on his acting career. In the face of mammoth tasks and seemingly insurmountable challenges, there is just one thing we can do: take one step at a time. For George, his single steps paved the way from classroom clown to BAFTA nominee and beyond. For me, each step took me closer to the next temple and the lessons it held.

What does this all mean for you? It's simple: once you have decided upon the work, career or business that you would really love to be your 'living', it is likely that the size of the task ahead may seem overwhelming. If so, just concentrate on the very next step ahead of you.

In the meantime, forget the 'big picture' of your grandest dreams and restrict your attention to the here and now, to the smallest step or action immediately in front of you. Don't worry that focusing on the mundane will stifle your creativity; it won't. A multitude of single steps lead to exotic and unseen lands. Life's heartbeat thumps as loudly in one step as it does in many.

Taking things step by step may mean that your departure from a job, about which you are ambivalent, towards a dream career will be gradual rather than immediate.

I have always been someone who has leapt, both feet first, towards my goals and desires, trusting that life will catch me in its invisible safety net. But this extreme method of change is not for everyone and, as with all things, there are many routes to success. George suggested a subtler (and more sensible) approach. 'Don't stop what you're doing. Don't cut the head off and expect the body to carry on living. Just make incremental changes,' he said.

'So, for example, at weekends in your time off, pursue your passion. See if you can start making a bit of money at it. See if people like what your passion is and see if you can start paying the bills from money made that way. Then increase it, increase it, increase it, until eventually there comes a time when you have to leave your present job.

'I think it's really important to do it in a way where you don't force yourself into financial dire straits.'

Great advice from someone who as 'been there, and done that'.

Let's take a look at an exercise that will help you think about those all-important small steps.

Take a sheet of paper and turn it so that it is in landscape position in front of you.

On the far left of the paper write where you are currently in terms of work, for example 'I'm working at Bartholomew's widget-making factory'.

On the far right of the paper, write where you ideally want to end up. Be brave, don't skimp on your ideals, for example, 'I am a best-selling, award-winning novelist being head-hunted by every publisher on the planet!'

Draw a straight line between the two.

Starting at your end goal, work backwards in steps:

- I am a best-selling, award-winning novelist.
- Get accepted by a publisher who loves my manuscript, supports me and has the ability to get my book to lots of readers.
- Get an agent who can find a publisher who is likely to love my manuscript.
- Research how to find an agent.
- Work on my manuscript so that is good enough to catch the eye of an agent.
- Sign up for a writing course on structure, dialogue and writing rhythm.

Can you see where this example is going? Have fun with this exercise; it's not an exact science because, of course, life can never be fully planned, but it will shake up your brain for creative answers.

Backtrack the steps until you arrive at something that you can do today, that will take you one step closer to your dream. That step could be as small as reading a blog post on creative writing, ordering a book about writing or simply writing a blog post yourself and learning as you go (something I recommend highly).

We all love the high that comes from completing a task, no matter how tiny. These small wins are addictive, in a positive way, and soon you will find that your consistent commitment to them will add up to become significant strides up the mountain of your desires.

Sometimes, however, even after embracing the idea of

'one-stepping', a problem arises: we find ourselves realising that, actually, we don't know what the next step might be. In this instance we will need the guidance of Lesson 3.

Lesson 3:
When the student is ready, the teacher appears

I unlocked the front door to an ominous silence. Our Jack Russell terrier, Smudge, was sitting on her hind legs staring up at me with wide eyes and a bemused look on her face. 'Hello?' I called out, unsure of the where-abouts of Sheri, my wife. After searching the places I usually find her when I get home, I did not expect the sight that greeted me.

Sheri was in our bedroom, sitting on the floor by the far side of the bed, crying into her hands. I didn't spot her at first; it was only Smudge who outed her when she jumped on the bed and barked in her direction. 'What on earth has happened?' I asked, worried and fearing the worst.

'I just don't know what to do,' sobbed Sheri.

The four stages of learning

The process of learning has been called different things

at different times. In 1969, management trainer Martin M. Broadwell referred to the stages of something called the 'psychology model'; then in 1970, the psychologist Noel Burch described the model as 'The four stages for learning any new skill' and began to use it while teaching business coaching in communication and human relations.

The psychology model comprises four stages through which we all pass when learning anything new. These are:

1. **Unconscious incompetence:**
   At this first stage, a person simply doesn't know what they don't know; they are wholly unaware of a deficit in knowledge, possibly not even conscious that acquisition of a new skill is necessary in the first place.

2. **Conscious incompetence:**
   At Stage 2 an individual recognises that they have deficient skills in a particular area and can understand the value of acquiring them. They now know what they don't know, and the journey of learning can begin.

3. **Conscious competence:**
   An individual knows how to do something, but being relatively early in their learning, they still require high levels of concentration to perform the skill. At this stage they can do it, it's just not yet natural.

4. **Unconscious competence:**
   An individual is so well versed in the skill that they can do it without thinking; not only that, they can also do it while executing another task. The skill is second nature. It's 'in the cells', so to speak. Now they are rolling.

When you enter a new world, environment, domain or career, you become a beginner again. The 88 Temple Pilgrimage, a circuitous rather than a linear pilgrimage (such as, for example, the Camino de Santiago), ends back at Ryozenji, Temple 1, where it all began. The symbolism of this cannot be overstated: at the end of one journey, as an adept, we begin another, as a novice. If we dare to recreate ourselves anew, then without exception this is the order of things. With the right attitude and understanding, it is also where the fun lies.

Sheri, head in hands, cried as she found herself suspended in limbo somewhere between the first two stages of the four stages of the learning model. She was a newbie in a new world, and she simply didn't know what she needed to do next. And it terrified her.

Sheri comes from a teaching background; both her parents were teachers and it was somewhat inevitable that she would follow in their footsteps, despite her perfunctory teenage resistance to carrying on the 'family business'.

'My mum kept saying, "you should be a teacher", and I said, "no, I don't want to be", Sheri explained.

'Then it came to work experience time, I was around sixteen or seventeen, and we all had to find a placement. I ended up being placed at a school called Northdene, where my mum was deputy head. I thought, "Oh well, I'll give it a go, it's only for two weeks."

'I ended up really enjoying it,' she admits, 'and they even allowed me to lead a class for a couple of days, when a teacher was ill.

'I started to think that, actually, this is what I should be doing. So, I applied for teacher training college, secured a place and, three years later, qualified as a teacher.'

Sheri then taught full-time for more than twenty years, working with a diverse range of people – mostly children – in different countries around the world, including South Africa, the United Arab Emirates and the UK. She has a way with teaching children that some refer to as a 'gift' and is one of those teachers who stays fondly embedded in a child's memory long into their adulthood (we all have one of those – mine was Mr Lee, my rugby teacher).

So it was a shock to her family when, not so long ago, she decided to change her career and become an artist.

'My mum had a meltdown when I told her I was leaving my teaching job,' Sheri said.

'I didn't study art at school, nothing meaningful anyway, but I was always fascinated by it,' she admits.

'Growing up, my family had a friend, a neighbour called Lynne Barry. I used to babysit her children as a child and later house-sat for them too. I knew Lynne was an artist and I enjoyed looking at some of her work around the house when I sat for them.

'One time, Lynne invited me to take part in a little eight-week art course that she was hosting at her house, and I decided to give it a go. At first I thought, "I'm not going to be any good at art," but I ended up doing some good pieces. More importantly, I really liked it.'

Although still in the early stages of her new life as an artist, Sheri shares a common trait with all the other Buddhist Millionaires in this book: she is willing to say 'yes' to the opportunities and new experiences that life offers, even without the assurance that she will succeed at them.

Impermanence

If you spend more than five minutes on any social-media platform, you will at some point have a meme like this show up in your feed or on your timeline: "This too will pass", "The only constant is change", "You can never step in the same river twice..." and so on. While almost all of these aphorisms end up being attributed to the wrong source, the sentiment is important nevertheless: that life is in constant flux. It is one of Buddhism's most essential teachings. The Buddhist teaching of impermanence (*mujō* in Japanese) teaches that all things, whether they be material or mental, are in a constant state of change between birth, growth, decay and death (and birth again in one form or another).

Whether one is Buddhist or not, it is an undeniable lesson that is easy to observe all around us almost all of the time: the changing of the seasons; the birth, life and death of friends and family; the blossom, flower, fruit and eventual apple core thrown into the recycling box at the end of lunch.

For Sheri Lennon, the first major change came when she was about 15 years into her teaching career.

'I had been teaching at the same school in London for all that time and, honestly, I had reached as far as I could go professionally.

'I received a telephone call from someone in Oman in the Middle East, asking if I would be interested in helping set up a handful of nurseries and pre-prep schools in Salalah, in the south of Oman. Apparently, I had been recommended for this because of my experience in early years education. So, I jumped at the opportunity. I felt it was time for a change.'

Sheri gave up her job in London and relocated to Oman ready to start her new project.

She knew that it was very different working in the Middle East, because her mum had worked there for fourteen years. Different cultures have different ways of operating and part of the enjoyment of working overseas is acclimatising to new procedures, policies and processes. 'But when I hadn't been paid after four months, alarm bells started to ring in my head', she said.

What followed was a protracted battle between Sheri

and her employer, simply to be paid. 'There came a time, almost six months in, where I had to cut my losses and return to the UK – without a penny in wages and in debt for rent, food and flights that I'd had to fund personally (with a little help from my husband), despite having been promised I would be reimbursed. I never was.'

Thankfully, her old school welcomed her back with open arms, happy to have their 'star' teacher return and keen to support the emotional bumps and bruises that she'd suffered from her experience.

'I was very grateful to the school and, understandably, knew that my original head of early years position couldn't be reinstated, as the vacant post had now been filled. So, I accepted a regular class teacher position. I loved it, initially.'

But as the saying suggests, it is indeed difficult to 'step in the same river twice', and retrograde steps, although taken with good intent, can often be harmful.

'I like being the boss, and having the freedom to govern myself and control my own affairs,' Sheri says.

'And though I was grateful to the school for allowing me to return, both they and I knew that it couldn't work for long – I remember my boss encouraging me to start out on my own. So, I did…'

So here she was, just six weeks into a bold plan to 'shake things up' and make a go of 'creating something from nothing'. She was going to make a living doing art.

Many people, including family members and close

friends, questioned her bold move, subtly suggesting that, maybe, she could start with something for which she was better suited.

'The thing is, I married this man about ten years ago,' she said, pointing to me with a wry smile, 'who lives by the philosophy that you should do what you love, and that it will always pay, eventually. It just seemed like the right time to be bold.'

The wall

There I was, staring down at Sheri, who was sitting head in hands, sobbing that she didn't know what to do next, and that it was my fault!

Sheri had hit the wall, just as many of those brave enough to step into the unknown undoubtedly do at some point. She had been buoyed up early on by the excitement and stimulation of new beginnings, but was now starting to comprehend that as a freshman, she simply didn't know what she needed to know to move up to the next rung of the ladder. She wasn't even certain what that next rung might be.

Life has a funny way of working out. It also has an uncanny way of providing the next piece of information just when you need it. I'm not really sure how this works, not scientifically anyway, but I have witnessed it enough times in both my own and others' lives, and with such consistency, to suggest that it is some type of 'law'.

While on my 88 Temple Pilgrimage, this law – that when the student is ready, the teacher will appear – manifested itself as literally as possible.

Like Sheri, I too had jumped into an environment about which I knew very little, other than that it was something that I desired. A few days into the pilgrimage, already exhausted from walking twelve hours a day and overwhelmed by the cultural saturation that can drown visitors to Japan, I stood in front of a temple and panicked a little.

What on earth did I hope to get out of this trip? I had flown nearly 6,000 miles to what exactly? What was the point of pilgrimage? Can it really change your life? How do you get the most out of it? Had I made a massive, overly romantic mistake in trusting that self-reflection could make a difference in a 21st-century world?

All my answers came from one man – Hajime San. Hajime appeared at my shoulder as I stood at that temple; and in just three short days taught me all I needed to know to make the rest of the 88 Temple Pilgrimage one of the most life-changing and affirming experiences I have ever had. Sheri was about to meet her teacher saviour also.

Let it come to you

One of the decisions Sheri made early on was to rent a small art studio so she could work freely without the blurred boundaries and distractions that often exist when working from home. She enjoyed setting up her space: putting her work on the walls; organising her workplace and meeting neighbouring artists.

Kjell Folkvord is an experienced Norwegian artist with a studio three doors down from Sheri. He is a kindly man with a warm smile, keen eye and, like many Scandinavians, a sharp wit. He helped welcome Sheri into her new art 'home-from-home' and they formed an instant friendship.

Several days after Sheri's dark moment of doubt, Kjell popped into her studio for an impromptu visit. He stood looking at her eclectic art adorning the walls and work spaces of her studio.

'You seem to be searching for your style,' Kjell said to her. 'Don't search for it, let it come to you.' His calming tone was enough to soothe Sheri's dented confidence somewhat, and she decided to keep working on her art, even signing up to participate in an upcoming annual art fair.

Weekend art fairs are fabulous events, but they entail long days, with an ebb and flow of viewers and customers throughout the Saturday and Sunday. Between the periods when hordes of people crowd an artist's stand, are times when there are none and not much to do. In one of these moments, Sheri decided to draw and colour some characters, just to pass the time.

She drew students and other people she knew, or had known; buildings she loved; animals from memories of childhood camping holidays in the Botswana bush with her family. She drew pictures, in abundance, of all manner of things. Unbeknown to her, a style was emerging in that weekend that people would pay handsomely for. Not only that, but it would also be the beginning of her career as a children's book illustrator.

Sheri had reached the wall before that weekend when she simply didn't know what would be her next step, and life, in its funny way, had provided an answer and direction.

It's impossible to predict how the help and guidance you need will appear, but it will appear. Once you realise that you don't know what your next step should be, and you have accepted that, life will show you it to you.

After a while, you'll begin to trust this process and lose some of the fear that comes from stepping into the unknown. Personally, I now actively seek to identify the things that I don't know in my life, to see where it takes me; you might find this following exercise helpful – it certainly has been for me.

What don't I know?

The purpose of this exercise is to help you establish the habit of actively seeking out, and even learning to enjoy, things that you don't know. For example, identify an area of your work life that is 'stuck'. Maybe you are experiencing lower than expected sales on a digital teaching programme that you developed and have absolutely no idea why. Maybe you keep getting passed over for promotion at your workplace even though you believe that it should be you moving up the career ladder. Maybe you keep losing out, at the very last stage, on that all-important part in a play, despite all the previous auditions going very well.

It doesn't matter what your problem is, and it doesn't matter that you don't yet know the answer. The skill you are trying to develop in this exercise is being honest about where you are (Lesson 1), and having the confidence to declare your ignorance (Lesson 3), so that the next step will be revealed (Lesson 2).

It's as though the declaration of our 'stuckness' – an acceptance that we don't yet have it all figured out – opens us to solutions. We can relax, no longer bound by the tension of needing to be right, and our new-found humility paves the way for guidance, in whatever form that takes. Once you have identified your 'stuck' areas:

1. Admit them to yourself.
2. Write them down.
3. Admit them to a friend or family member.
4. Wait patiently, relax and 'listen' for solutions or answers to appear.

Lesson 4:
The 'to-don't' list –
the art of effortlessness

I have some fantastic news: life is going to do its thing, with or without your interference. Don't believe me? Try and memorise the more than 500 functions of your liver for yourself; see how successful you will be at guaranteeing perfect weather for your summer barbecue; see how the weeds keep growing in your garden, despite many hours spent removing them.

The lesson of this chapter is one of the most important, and if you embrace it, you will enjoy your route to work success so much more than if you tried to micromanage your way through the experience.

The lesson is simple (though not to be confused with easy). It is this: don't try too hard to achieve your work goals. Actually, this is the negative iteration of the lesson; the positive version is: relax, let go, enjoy the journey and trust that you'll get where you want to go, sooner or later.

In today's environment, as we have seen, hard work, ambition, determination, scholastic endeavour and sacrifice (to the cause) are not only admired, but expected.

Test this for yourself. Ask someone you know, whom you recognise to be 'stressed' or just 'a bit uptight', about their plans for the forthcoming day. This person is likely to babble on about a whole list of 'to-dos' from a list either written down or in their head. These people are busy being busy, and many of us are guilty of this. It's as if by crashing our way through a colossal list of mundane tasks, we can gain some measure of self-worth with our self-flagellating efforts. We take pride in our busyness even if it's not the greatest way to do business.

Think of some of the phrases that many of us grew up listening to and learning from: 'no pain, no gain'; 'money doesn't grow on trees'; 'stop daydreaming, be realistic'; 'work harder'. We all know these admonishments or variations of them. The implication is that hard work and effort will reap rewards, while daydreaming and creative pursuits are better left to be enjoyed on rainy days (another way of saying that they are lazy ideals).

While any journey of success will most certainly involve massive effort, we can ease the burden by working not harder, but more smartly.

Many of the people interviewed for this book exhibit, to varying degrees, the lesson that less is more. None more so than Charles Negromonte.

The gentle art

Charles is a handsome, square-jawed 27-year-old from Paulista, a small coastal town on the east coast of Brazil. He looks ferociously strong, and he is, but this is not what is most impressive about him. It's the way he doesn't use his strength that's notable.

Charles is a world-class competitor and teacher of Brazilian jiu jitsu, a grappling-based martial art of Japanese origin, practised by many Brazilians.* He too has been brave enough to place passion before profit and, in return, life has provided him with the opportunity to make a career from doing so.

'When I decided to do what I do [jiu jitsu], although I had the support of everyone it was a long time of making no money,' said Charles in his broad Brazilian accent, still sweating after coming off the jiu jitsu mats to grant me an interview.

'But what I do is something way bigger than just a means of earning money. I fell in love with it and I don't see myself going to work nine-to-five every day. When I

---

* In 1914, Japanese judo and jiu jitsu expert Mitsuo Maeda travelled to Brazil, where he befriended a businessman named Gastão Gracie. Maeda taught the skills of the art to Gracie's son, Carlos, who continued to pass them on to other family members. With every iteration from Maeda to Gastão to Carlos and beyond, the techniques became a little more 'Brazilian'. And so Brazilian jiu jitsu was born.

was a teenager, I said to myself, "I don't want to have this life, the nine-to-five, I need to find a different way." And then I found it [jiu jitsu], and the money was something that came after many years.'

Making money from a sport or martial art such as jiu jitsu is not easy. There are two main streams of possible income: from teaching and/or from competing. It often takes many years to establish both the skills and the platform necessary to be successful in either one. Many give up long before their dream of making their living in such a niche area has been realised. But not Charles. His unshakeable commitment to creating a life he treasures has been, it seems, worth the years of effort.

'I love to teach, but I think the most important part of this whole journey is the quality of life you have. For some people who work nine-to-five every day, they have jobs they don't love to do. I think they have a sad feeling and hardship inside.

'Life's so short, and then you work most of your life doing something you don't love. I don't get it. I see people every day coming in and complaining about their job. Even people who make lots of money, they complain, they still complain! And the year's passing, and they still complain! But they do nothing to change,' Charles told me.

Although this chapter focuses on the art of effortlessness, there is no getting away from the fact that massive amounts of effort are still needed to be successful in life.

Clearly it is not easy for an average-sized baby to squeeze its way out of a not-nearly-wide-enough birth canal in order to take its first breath (I think most mothers would agree). And it is no more easy for a tender shoot to fight its way through the concrete slabs that pave over its access to light. My point is not that life is not hard work; my point is that we don't need to make it harder than it already is.

Our proclivity for trying to control outcomes that are beyond our control is futile. Contriving solutions, working harder than necessary or simply going against the natural order will make a situation worse – or, at the very least, waste time and energy.

This is plain to see when watching Charles compete or teach jiu jitsu to beginners.

The name jiu jitsu translates as 'the gentle art'. As with all Japanese translations, it is necessary to look beyond the surface meaning to fully understand the nuance. While further investigation into the word *jitsu* offers only two possible translations with similar meaning ('art' or 'technique'), other translations of *jiu* are more revealing.

As well as meaning 'gentle', the *jiu* of jiu jitsu can also mean 'soft', 'supple', 'flexible', 'pliable', or 'yielding'; all words that stand in opposing corners to the 'no pain, no gain' and 'train harder, be stronger' methodologies practiced by martial arts devotees, and also many of us. You can see this contrast playing out when a beginner takes their first tentative steps onto the jiu jitsu training mats.

I'll give you a quick whistle-stop tour of the art so you

can understand better what I will be talking about and, more importantly, I will show how this is relevant knowledge for securing or creating meaningful work that pays well (and no, it doesn't involve attacking your boss!).

There is no punching, kicking or any other form of striking in jiu jitsu. It is an art of leverage in which it is possible, given the right skills and tactics, for the weak to overcome the strong.

But how is this possible? By pitching your full weight against the weak links of the human body chain.

The two most susceptible areas to attack are the joints and the neck. Hyper-extending a joint (bending it in the opposite direction to which nature intended), causing the occlusion of the carotid arteries (causing temporary unconsciousness by blocking blood flow, via the neck, to the brain), takes remarkably little effort* and it is what allows David to topple Goliath, so to speak. In all things jiu jitsu, it's not about your size, but about how you use your size. And beginners struggle to understand this early on .

You can always tell a beginner in a jiu jitsu class. They are the ones who, when paired with a smaller person, try their utmost to dominate with their size until, green from

---

* Which is why the first thing all jiu jitsu students learn is to honour the 'tap' – a universal indicator of submission whereby a jiu jitsu player alerts his partner/opponent *before* a technique reaches maximum extension or compression, thereby avoiding injury. This is done by either loudly tapping the ground or opponent with an available limb or, failing that, saying the word 'TAP'.

fatigue, they are forced to rest at the side before vomiting with exhaustion.

Such is their commitment to 'training hard' and 'powering through' that they fail to hear the wisdom of instructors, like Charles Negromonte, when they call out to them: 'relax guys'; 'less is more'; 'try to use your weight, not your strength'; 'play smart not hard'. Jiu jitsu is an art of leverage, it's the 'gentle art'.

In time all beginners, if they stay in the game long enough to understand the futility of working too hard, learn to use leverage instead of power. And it is the same for all of us who start out on a new path towards our ideal work life.

Not nothing

It's easy to mistake effortlessness for doing nothing. But there is still much to do to reach the destinations we have set ourselves. We are not doing nothing to achieve our ends.

I heard the following story from a church pastor many years ago, while visiting a friend in South Carolina. It helps demonstrate my point.

There was a pious man, Burt, who lived in his home in the bayous of Florida. One day, a violent storm flooded the local rivers and marshes and Burt's garden. A concerned neighbour telephoned and said to him: 'Burt, why don't you get out of town. Go stay at your sister's until the storm stops.'

'I'll be okay,' answered Burt. 'It doesn't look like this storm will be much and, besides, you know I am a God-fearing man and God, he'll look after me.'

The rains continued to fall through the night, and the next morning Burt's basement and ground floor became flooded. He saved what furniture he could by taking it upstairs to the bedroom.

'Burt,' called the local sheriff from the cab of his 4x4 vehicle, which he'd pulled up on a dry verge of a neighbouring property, 'grab some clothes! I'll take you to your sister's – this storm ain't getting any better.'

'Come now, sheriff,' called back Burt from his bedroom window, 'you know this storm will pass, happens every year 'bout this time and, besides, you know I am a God-fearing man and God, he'll look after me.'

The next morning, Burt woke to water lapping at his toes. He scrambled out of the window onto the roof.

'Mr Johnson,' insisted the crew of a rescue recovery boat, 'you must come with us, sir. We need to evacuate this storm zone.'

'Boys, y'all a bit wet behind the ears, this is the bayou – we made of sterner stuff, and besides, I'm a God-fearing man and God, he'll look after me.'

As the water continued to rise, Burt sat on his roof hugging his knees to his chest. He waved away the helicopter as it dangled down a rope ladder for him. Over the din of the whirring blades, the pilot couldn't hear Burt say; 'Now off you go with your 'copter, don't you know

I'm a God-fearing man and God, he'll look after me.'

Burt drowned.

At the gates of St Peter, Burt yelled at God: 'How could you? I've been a God-fearing man my whole life; I pray, I believe and still you didn't save me.'

To which God answered gently: 'Burt, I gave you a brain, sent you a friend, then a sheriff, a rescue boat and even a helicopter…'

It is dangerously easy to mistake non-action for no action. This needs to be thoroughly understood before we can successfully create our ideal work.

To return to the mats of jiu jitsu, Charles Negromonte doesn't advocate doing nothing to his beginner students. Rather, he tutors them to do 'just enough; not more, not less'.

The importance of this approach is demonstrated by the potentially dangerous and dominating jiu jitsu position called 'Mount', in which the attacker straddles the defender, who is lying flat on their back, and sits heavily on either their chest or belly. It is one of the worst positions for a defender; trapped beneath the weight of an attacker with the potential, were it allowed, to rain down punches.*

---

* Although striking is not allowed in Brazilian jiu jitsu, it must be noted that what is now sport began as a martial art, designed to defend against all manner of attack – including punches. Teachers, while not permitting strikes, will frame a technique or tactic around its potential for self-defence should a 'real' fight ensue.

The beginner's tendency, under the weight and pressure of someone sitting heavily on their chest, is to try and muscle their way out of the problem. They huff and puff and attempt to push away the full weight of their opponent, using just their arms. This expends a massive amount of effort and energy for almost zero return. Despite their hard work, the attacker remains in a dominant position and the defender is left exhausted. They are working hard, not smart.

Once beginners have started to understand the concept of leverage that underpins the art of jiu jitsu, the defender will approach the 'Mount' problem in a very different way. Instead of attempting to push the attacker away using relatively weak body parts (the arms), they might subtly push out one of his or her straddling knees with their elbow (the short 'lever' of an elbow is stronger than the long lever of an arm due to its proximity to larger and stronger muscle groups), and insert a knee that will rest between themselves and the weight of the attacker.

This fairly simple move, with minimal effort, removes almost 70% of the weight pressure that the attacker previously was able to employ. Sensing that their attack has been somewhat thwarted, the attacker is forced to rethink their plan, dismount and try another technique. The defender is free, for now at least. They have worked smart, not hard.

Trust

Why do we try too hard? Why do we micromanage? Why do we work so hard to try and control the outcome of life? Why do we doubt with such fervour? I have thought about this for many years, and thought about it even more while on the 88 Temple Pilgrimage.

Walking for twelve hours or more a day while on pilgrimage with no smart phones, iPods, laptops or any other technological distractions, you fully 'see yourself'. By this I mean that with little else to do but walk, eat and sleep, you will come face to face with the thoughts in your head.

These thoughts are always present, whether we are on pilgrimage or during the humdrum of everyday living, but on pilgrimage, with so little distraction, they play out in Technicolor with Dolby surround sound. When you are quiet, you can at last hear the noise. Meditation has much the same effect; in fact, pilgrimage is simply another form of meditation. We'll look deeper into the art of meditation in the next chapter.

When you first observe how 'chatty' the mind is, it can be somewhat disconcerting, but at least you are now one step ahead of 'not knowing what you don't know'. Before you were too busy to notice the congestion and conflict going on between your ears.

With time, as you stay unflinchingly with your thought debris, it begins to settle of its own accord. Like wild animals, thoughts don't want trouble. If you leave them alone, they will leave you alone, only reacting if you poke them with a stick or try and put them in a box. Leave the thoughts alone, and they will move on by. Let bygones be bygones.

The space left between new and vacating thoughts is where insight (and our 'personal power', which we'll also cover later) can be found. In one such moment I was moved to write these two journal entries while on a pilgrimage:

> Trust means to let go.
> Don't walk to the temple, let the temple come to you.

Both of these thoughts came in response to my ponderings on why we all tend to try too hard. On reflection, both suggest we should trust that life has got 'stuff covered'. Can you believe this? Can you trust in that idea? Can you entertain that life, with or without your interference, has got your back?

It's hard to do. I quite understand, I am a controller at heart and I feel your pain. It's particularly challenging when we are not quite sure 'what' or 'who' has got our backs in this game of life. Is it Nature, God, the universe, Buddha, divine intervention, aliens – what?

As I have already mentioned, many people are drawn to Buddhist teachings because of their insistence on experience over faith. Buddhism suggests you find confidence in evidence-based or personal experience, not the blind following of another's doctrine.

Try this exercise: write down ten things which, although you might not know how they work, do work. For example, I have no concrete idea how my laptop performs all its functions, but here I am typing on it. I also don't know conclusively, despite the many and varied theories, how life and our universe began, but I know it did – because I'm here, in a universe that has been born, typing on a laptop, the workings of which I don't fully understand!

We don't need to know how something works to enjoy its benefits.

Of course, education and understanding go a long way to building trust and faith in any given subject, and one of the goals of this book is to provide both, but they are not necessary. More valuable is building your own experiences and examples that prove to you that less is more. Collate your own portfolio of evidence that demonstrates that by relaxing and trusting (in whatever source), all will be well.

Interfering busybody

Just before writing my journal entry, 'Don't walk to the temple, let the temple come to you', I had been working way too hard to achieve my goal.

To prove that time and money were self-created obstacles rather than universal truths I had decided to walk a 1,400km pilgrimage in just 30 days with virtually no money (£300 worth of yen was all I had in the bank at the time). I had neither enough time nor enough money to finish a journey that ordinarily should take months and require a budget five times bigger than mine, in order to stay safe, fed and housed in the evenings between days of walking.

My theory was that if I could complete a herculean task without sufficient time or money, then I could demonstrate that, contrary to popular belief, something other than time and money was the ultimate source of success. If I couldn't, then they were.

It's a depressing thought that time and money are the be-all and end-all of life. This idea has shaped our modern economy and we can all see what trouble it has got us into! Nevertheless, many times throughout the pilgrimage, I was seriously concerned that, unfortunately, it may be true. There were just too many kilometres to walk, in too little time, with not enough money to feed the energy expenditure necessary for the challenge.

So, I started to micromanage.

I began to do what so many of you will be tempted to do when moving towards the goal of creating your ideal work life. I started to 'take control', 'push further' and 'work harder'.

I started to walk faster so that I could cover more distance in a shorter time. I took fewer food and toilet breaks, so that I could spend more time pounding the road. I stopped talking to people along the way and enjoying the rare and fleeting communion that comes on pilgrimage. Instead, I put my head down and drove on, fully focused on the finish line.

Did it help? Of course not. In fact, it made things worse. The lack of food, extra walking speed, stress and strain hardened my plight. I lost a full day of walking and almost the rest of my budget paying for a room in a *ryokan* (a traditional Japanese inn), when I was forced to sleep for almost 24 hours to recover from the extra effort. I was broken. As it turned out, I wasn't able to micromanage the universe and control the circumstances of life. My extra effort took me no closer to the finish line. Who would have guessed?

Learning to let go is difficult, I'm not suggesting otherwise, but we take an important step if we recognise that it is a skill we need to develop.

Do you remember learning to walk? You will have started as a nervous toddler, stiff as a robot, clumsy and awkward, toppling every few steps with an unceremonious bump on your bottom. Now, as an experienced walker, you'll hardly realise that every day you are successfully carrying out a set of complex skills that allow you to effortlessly perform something that was once seemingly impossible.

Much of this learning is a natural cognitive process wired into our brain's mechanics. Early skills are filtered through our prefrontal cortex (our thinking, conscious brain), until, on mastery, they are stored in our limbic brain (automatic subconscious brain). The prefrontal cortex is freed for further new skills, learning and growth.

Although this process is inherent and beyond our total control, we can shorten the time it takes to master a skill or achieve a goal. By simply paying attention to the added tension of 'overtrying' as we learn, and actively reminding ourselves to 'let go', 'relax', 'soften' and 'drop the strain', we allow our subconscious to guide our actions unimpinged.

As you gain confidence in this process, you will start to see that the conscious thinking brain has just one simple task: to identify what you want. That's basically it. After goal selection, it can go for a lie-down, while other brain systems go about the hard work of putting together the jigsaw of our desires.

Here's a trip down memory lane: remember flicking through the retail catalogue as a child in December, ahead of Christmas? 'I want that, ooh that too; a couple of those; how great would it be to have one of those?' That's the job of the conscious brain. To identify and choose what we would love to be, do or have.

Once you have chosen your heart's desire, the hardest part is staying out of your own way long enough to let your subconscious do what it is designed to do. It would be ludicrous to dig up the seeds of an oak tree every few minutes to check that the natural process was taking place – in fact this interference would be a guaranteed way to kill the oak before it had a chance to root. Yet this is what we often do with our personal goals and choices: we make a choice, then we either micromanage and interfere, or at the first sign of hardship or when our patience is tested, we review our goals for those with less ambition.

Why do we do this? Maybe it's because we don't trust that our deepest wishes and desires will be manifest, pure and simple. If someone or something could guarantee that all of your goals would be achieved, you would never fear and you would never interfere with the goals you had originally set. After we have dared to uncover and admit to ourselves our deepest passion, that which we would love to make our work and career, the majority of work on the path of the Buddhist Millionaire is learning to stay out of your own way while the universe does its thing.

The 'to-don't' list exercise

We all have a 'to-do' list; there isn't a person alive in modern society who doesn't have one stacked with chores. But this exercise will help you develop a 'to-don't' list instead. We'll use this to build your confidence, one step at a time, in the reality that life has a way of helping you get where you need to be.

Firstly, pick something on your 'to-do' list. Just something little, start small. Transfer this to your 'to-don't' list.

Now, whatever you have chosen, achieve it with as little of your own effort as possible. Hand over the effort to the universe/aliens/subconscious, and just observe what happens.

Allow me to use a pet hate chore as an example: cleaning my office.

If I'm not careful I have a tendency, once I start my office sort-out, to become maniacal; a sort of Tasmanian devil of tidying. Rabid with organising fever, instead of just sorting the basics, I often move on to invoice filing, bookshelf straightening, flaky paint stripping, cobweb dusting...

I end up turning a necessary but quick job into a marathon task that eats into the rest of the day, tires me out and, more often than not, makes me grumpy, as I realise how much time and energy I've lost cleaning and not dealing with other important things. So instead, after recognising that I have become overambitious, I take a five-minute 'to-do' list hiatus. I leave the room, make a cup of tea and literally force myself to STOP.

After five minutes or so, once I've found my calm within the storm, I go back to the original task.

Refreshed and calmer, I can see that I'm doing more than I need or that it might be wiser to spread the workload of office organisation over three days – twenty minutes focused tidying per day – rather than a five-hour maelstrom of busy-beeing that more often than not leads me nowhere. Small wins with energy to spare feel just as good, if not better, than big exhausting gains.

Not only that but I have found that, strangely, when I give up trying too hard and micromanaging my life, things tend to fall into place by themselves. Out of the blue my wife may pop her head around the door and ask if I would like some help, or the pile of papers that needs to be filed turns out to be mostly junk mail that can be chucked in the bin. Who knows what coincidences will manifest for you if you work smart. You'll have to find out for yourself, but as a happy observer of serendipity in my own life, I can confidently suggest that you will experience the same in yours.

If it helps, keep this mantra in mind:

Don't do less than enough. Don't do more than enough.
Just do enough.

This is not quite as easy as it sounds. You will, more than likely, be tempted to overdo it. Don't worry – if this happens, just keep reminding yourself that the goal is to practise the art of 'less is more', and get back to working smart, not hard.

When a 'to-do' on your 'to-don't' list gets done, simply cross it off, note the success, congratulate yourself for not trying, and move on to the next one!

When do you know you are trying too hard?

By now I hope you are recognising the importance of getting out of your own way in regard to goal achievement. It's not that the subconscious and the other goal-creating systems working on your behalf care much about your interference; they will continue to do their part regardless. It will simply be a more pleasant journey if you sit back, smell the roses along the way and let the uncontrollable do what it's designed to do.

Yet sometimes, despite not wanting to interfere, we can't help ourselves! And it is important to recognise the difference between action (those single progressive steps that we are taught to take to get us from point A to point B) and micromanaging.

I asked one of our Buddhist Millionaires, Ian McClelland, how to recognise when your ego is interfering and you are in danger of self-sabotaging your cause.

'When it stops being fun,' was his succinct and perfect reply.

We can use McClelland's wise observation to check in and see if we are working hard or smart. Try this:

In times of quiet, maybe when you are taking a relaxing bath or just before you drift off to sleep at night, think about the goal or task that you have set out to achieve. Now 'listen'.

'Listen' to how your body, thoughts and feelings respond. If you immediately feel a sense of tightness, possibly combined with actual muscle tension (check your jaw, bottom and shoulders), and your heart begins to accelerate to the beat of your over thinking mind, chances are that you are chasing your passion too hard and it is causing stress.

On the other hand, if musing on your goals creates feelings of ease, relief, excitement and a hopeful glow, you are probably going about your business in the 'zone'. Easy.

Effortless. Joyful. Enjoying every minute of it.

What we feel in our bodies is a perfect indicator of what we feel in our minds about something. We can ignore these emotions, but we can never deny them. They are an important alarm system for our lives.

If you do find that thinking about your goals creates feelings of tension rather than ease, you will most certainly want to read the next chapter, Lesson 5.

Lesson 5:
The art of meditation – connecting to your personal power supply

'Don't aim at success – the more you aim at it and make it a target, the more you are going to miss it. For success, like happiness, cannot be pursued...'

– Viktor E. Frankl,
Man's Search for Meaning

All the lessons on the path of the Buddhist Millionaire in some way overlap. They all facilitate and support each other, and none more so than this one and the previous lone. The art of meditation and 'not trying too hard' are one and the same. In fact, 'letting go' is one of the skills that meditation teachers try to impart.

Today, most people are familiar, at least, with the term meditation. It has become something of a 'trending' activity, and while it is to be welcomed that instruction in this art has filtered down from the cloud-shrouded temples of far-off lands, I fear that some of its more significant benefits have been lost in translation.

Certainly, it has been scientifically proven that regular meditation is good for the health, but there are additional, greater benefits beyond this. One of these is that it can help you shape a profitable and enjoyable work-life, which, considering we spend a third of our lives working, is no mean feat.

The three schools of meditation

Although Buddhism teaches that the historical Buddha taught over 10,000 ways to meditate, generally speaking there are just three main schools of meditation: Vipassana, Tibetan and Zen.

Vipassana focuses on mindfulness and insight; Tibetan uses guided imagery techniques while Zen mixes 'sitting still doing nothing' with trying to solve brain-scrambling riddles (*koans*) such as: 'What is the sound of one hand clapping?'

Although I have now tried all three, my meditation practice began over 25 years ago at a Tibetan school based in London. I can still remember my teacher's bright eyes, wide smile and short legs folded beneath him as he advised his congregation to simply 'Drop it!' (excessive thinking, that is).

You don't really need to understand the history of each school or differences between their techniques to assist you with the task here at hand. Of course, you may feel moved to investigate further in your own time, but for now I'm going to teach what will be immediately applicable and useful.

Meditation is frequently cloaked in unnecessary mysticism, making it inaccessible to many. However, this is often just an attempt to explain the inexplicable. Meditation is simply a skill, and like all skills, it takes practice to master and fully appreciate its value.

You are going to use the skill of meditation to help clear away the brambles of scattered, runaway thoughts in order to access deeper recesses of focused, directed thinking. With this clearer thinking, it will be easier not only to identify what work you really want to do, irrespective of pay (if you haven't already done so), but also to tap into the inner resources available, at this deeper state, that will help you achieve such a goal.

Deep work

'Deep work' is the term that author and computer science professor, Cal Newport, coins to explain further the work of Carl Jung, the founder of analytical psychology, who was also influential in the fields of psychiatry, anthropology, archaeology, literature, philosophy and religious studies.

Jung was a great believer in the powers of meditation. a stone retreat, 'Bollingen Tower' where, it is said, he would often retire both to meditate and focus fully on challenging work projects.

Similarly, Albert Einstein, was reported to seek silent solitude to foster insight and intellectual breakthroughs.

Imagine Einstein standing, chalk in hand, and staring at a blackboard full of mathematical calculations. For hours, days, weeks, months and years on end he stands and stares while algebraic symbols course through his mind until – eureka – he has the answer he was searching for.

Did Einstein find the answer or did the answer find Einstein?

In modern Western living, we are taught from an early age that hard work pays off, and that we are the creators of our own future and fortune. While this may be partly true, there is an essential element missing from this success-creating equation. We may not be in the driving seat as much as we have been led to believe.

Albert Einstein could not force a correct answer from his mind any more than you or I can force one from ours. What is essential, is to create an environment, where we can 'see' the answers as they bubble up from the deepest recesses of our consciousness.

Accessing the best parts of ourselves, the parts that are going to manage a fulfilling, fun and profitable work life, won't be achieved by doing things, but by not doing things, the way the Zen Buddhists do – or don't, as the case may be!

Two techniques

Few of us regularly, if ever, access our deepest inner resources. I'm going to teach you two techniques, from my own direct experience, which I have found to be beneficial in carving out my own life as a Buddhist Millionaire.

Technique 1 – muddy focus:

Think of a laser beam: light particles so tightly packed together that, when focused on a single area of an absorbent surface, they can produce enough heat to start a fire. In contrast, if the light particles are dissipated and unfocused, the essential heat required to make fire is scattered and lost. Our minds work in much the same way.

Meditation is simply the practice of building a laser focus rather than allowing distracted ineffectiveness. For some of us, sometimes, the mind is so distracted that we need an 'anchor' with which to steady our busy brain.

For the following exercise, our anchor is going to be a pot of muddy water. Here are the instructions:

1. Fill a lidded glass jar with water and add one tablespoon of mud. Screw the lid tightly shut.
2. Sit down in front of the jar, don't slouch and keep

your back straight (we may as well work on your posture as well as your meditation!).

3. Shake the jar.
4. Watch as the mud slowly settles to the bottom.
5. Keep watching, as it will continue to settle.
6. I said, keep watching!
7. When all the mud has settled and the water is clear (ish), your meditation practice is done – for now!

This exercise can take anything from five to ten minutes, depending on the size of the jar.

It is more than likely that your mind will wander from watching the mud and shift its attention to whatever unrelated thought has popped into your head at the time. Don't be concerned about this. Part of the focus developed through meditation is achieved by recognising that your mind has gone MIA (Missing In Action); this itself is a form of attentiveness. When you realise you have lost focus, gently bring your mind back to the task at hand – mud watching – with no self-recrimination.

At this point, we also need to discuss good habits.

There have been a number of excellent books written about the importance of good-habit creation with regard to achieving goals successfully. Two that come to mind are *Atomic Habits* by James Clear and *The Power of Habit* by Charles Duhigg.

The scientific findings in these books validate what Buddhists have said for decades and what we have all suspected to be true: good, consistent working habits lead to good results. Go figure!

If you are going to use meditation to help you achieve your work, career and life goals then you are going to have to begin, *and then maintain* such a practice.

Here's what I suggest, based on what has worked for me and others. Create a space that is your designated 'quiet space', and make sure it is approved by whoever lives with you (including the dog). Mine is in the bedroom, on my side of the bed. Ensure that it is a definable area in which you can do your meditation practice; somewhere distinct from other places in the house where different activities occur.

In my definable space stands a Buddha statue (absolutely not necessary for meditation – but I happen to be partial to a Buddha statue), framed photos of my son, daughter and wife, a few little trinkets gathered from various trips around the world, candles and an incense burner (again not necessary but I fell in love with the incense smell – *mainichi kō* – that wafts inside all of the 88 temples of the pilgrimage). This is your space. This is where you will practise in quiet solitude.

Now that you have somewhere to meditate, it's advisable to set a schedule for when you will do so. All the research suggests that regular, consistent habits and practice yield the best results, and I have also found this to be true.

While schedules can be fluid, to avoid disrupting your

regular meditation practice, try to find a time slot in the day that you are unlikely to change. I practise immediately on waking, while everyone is still in bed, and again just before bedtime, as I have found these times of day suffer the least disruption in terms of sudden changes to schedule.

Furthering your practice – the 'Russian doll' technique

As you progress with your practice, you will find it easier both to notice when your mind has strayed from mud watching and to bring it back to the task when it does. At this stage you will be ready to add another level of challenge and difficulty.

Think of a Russian doll: those intricately decorated, wooden toys that are opened to reveal another, slightly smaller one inside; then another; and another; and another, culminating in a teeny-weeny figure at the final opening. In this same way, but in reverse, let's build upon your muddy jar meditation technique.

You will need five jars of increasing size, placed in order, small to large.

Fill the smallest with mud and water as before, and continue your practice for two weeks. Then repeat using the next-size jar and continue in this way until you reach the largest jar, changing the size of jar every fortnight.

As you move up through the jars, the mud will take

longer to settle and you, in turn, will have increased your time meditating and improved your powers of focus.

Eventually, you will be able to focus on your practice for a solid 45 minutes or so.

Then the fun begins.

Technique 2 – red tomatoes

The benefits of your improved focus in meditation will begin to spill over into the rest of your life; after all, the mind being disciplined in your designated quiet space is the same one you take with you when you re-enter the regular world.

For example, you might find that practising meditation on rising sets a good tone for the day to come. How often have you noticed that like attracts like? When we are in high spirits, life seems to go our way; when miserable, it appears only to get worse.

You may experience another benefit if you meditate just before bedtime. Many people report they sleep much better after meditation and the benefits of a good night's sleep, for both health and productivity, are well documented.

Let's now look at a much more direct and obvious way of using the focus developed in meditation to affect both your work and work goals, directly. This is called the 'Pomodoro' technique, or in English, the 'Red Tomato' technique.

I must now apologise to whoever originally taught me this technique, because I cannot remember who it was! All I know is that it revolutionised my work as a writer and that of many others to whom I've recommended it.

The technique is essentially a work-based version of meditation, a way to do 'deep work' to use Newport's term again.

Here are the instructions:

1. Choose a work task that needs to be done: finishing the chapter of a book; completing a painting; organising your CV; drafting a business plan.
2. Find a space to work, free from distraction: free of people and things like social media, phone and email interruptions – much like your meditation space (although, I recommend, *not* your meditation space).
3. Set a timer for 30 minutes.
4. Work completely undistracted and uninterrupted for the full 30 minutes.
5. When the timer signals the end of the session, rest for two minutes. And do rest. Leave the space and do something totally different, or nothing at all, but don't work. Give the brain a breather.
6. Repeat steps 3–5 three more times until you have completed four 30-minute sessions, or one complete 'Pomodoro' (the four 30-minute sessions suggesting the four quarters into which a tomato is often cut).

As you become accustomed to this disciplined and highly focused way of working, you will notice not only an increase in concentration, but also in productivity and creativity.

And some other very bizarre phenomena...

Mind bending, time bending

There are, of course, ways other than the Pomodoro to dip into this 'deep-work' state. It also happens when walking a pilgrimage.

The temples of the 88 Temple Pilgrimage are not evenly spaced. For example, in the first three days you visit around ten that are clustered together in close proximity, while at other times it takes three or four days to walk from one temple to the next.

It was during one of these mind-bendingly long, hard and boring stretches of walk that I fell into a meditative state – a type of 'deep work', if you like.

On the morning that I set out on this marathon of a walk, I was resigned to the difficult days ahead. I had given up complaining and resisting the challenge, reminding myself instead simply to focus on the here and now, no matter how monotonous. If my mind drifted to thoughts of the finish line, I gently pulled it back to the walking.

As the miles wore on, my mind seemed to drop into the rhythm of my steps and invading and extraneous thoughts just gave up the ghost and stopped. I remember in their place, a profound sense of ease and calm. And yet, strangely, no matter how pleasant the feelings, I was neither attached nor too bothered about them; they were neither good, nor bad, they just 'were'. I was fully engaged in the moment and the task at hand and superfluous thought and judgement rolled off my mind like water off a duck's back.

The next moment, or so it seemed, a chill in the air cut into my mental state and I looked up to see the moon shining against the inky dark of a night sky. I had walked for almost fourteen hours without rest, yet it had seemed to me to be no more than 30 minutes. It was as if time had bent.

Meditators and others involved in focused work for long periods often report this distortion of time. In and of itself, it doesn't serve us much more than to provide an interesting anecdote for the pub when out with friends. But there is something else about this hyper-focused state that is directly beneficial to our immediate cause, as walkers on the path of the Buddhist Millionaire.

In this deep and profound state of hyper-focus, free from neurotic thinking, we get a glimmer of what the Buddhists call 'emptiness', and, paradoxically, it is full of potential.

Sitting still, and the art of 'emptiness'

As we've seen, both the 'Muddy Focus' and the 'Red

Tomato' techniques are extremely useful for improving focus and productivity. They are down-to-earth and practical tools that will help you contend with the day-to-day steps and actions necessary for creating joyful and productive work.

But there is more to life than the practical and the mundane. One of the gifts of the Buddhist way and, in turn, the way of the Buddhist Millionaire, is that it deals with both the mundane and the sacred. Used correctly, the sacred can genuinely and realistically influence the mundane.

When a new white-belt martial-arts student steps into a dojo (a traditional Japanese martial arts-training hall), they often stare in awe at the skills of the black belts in the class.

The gap between skill sets is so wide that, to the white belts, the black belts seem to have an almost mystical and magical quality. But as the years pass by, and the novice becomes the intermediate, not only does the skills gap reduce, but truth also dawns. The students realise that what once seemed magical is in fact the product of many hours of mundane effort. The magic is that there is no magic.

This next method of meditation is going to help you access the magic that is not magic – 'emptiness'.

Buddhists don't believe in a separate and benevolent creator or god figure. Rather, they believe that we are very much in charge and responsible for what happens in our life, and this is explained in the 'dependent origination' doctrine.

'Dependent origination' teaches that nothing exists on its own but derives from earlier circumstances. Everything is supported by something else in the past and provides support for something yet to come.

For example, a piece of paper is not conjured out of thin air by a creator. It is made from water and pulp. The wood comes from trees, which have come from seeds from other trees. In this way, everything has both a cause and an effect.

The concept of 'emptiness' in Buddhism takes this thought further. If nothing can exist as separate from something else then, at our source, we must all be one. We are literally part of the same source: that is the stars and the moon and everything in between.

Think about it another way – I like to call it 'unpeeling'.

Look at your hand – it certainly seems a definitive and specific thing. But imagine that you could unpeel what you see, pull back and discover what's underneath. When you pull back the skin on your hand, you find tendons, muscle and bone. When you pull back tendons, muscle and bone, you find blood, capillaries and cells. When you pull back cells, you find molecules, atoms, protons, electrons and so on.

Can you see where this is taking us?

Whatever other myriad steps that may be discovered

and named along the way, ultimately, we end up at a single source that holds all things.

This is 'emptiness'. Nothing can exist as separate from this. How could it? Where would it reside, itself held by the 'thing that holds all things'? Stay with this thought. It makes sense, given time.

Yet this 'emptiness' is not void of value. It is a tightly packed emptiness filled with everything there ever was, is, or will be. It is the ultimate power supply.

The idea of 'emptiness' often terrifies people, as it did me when I first heard Buddhists speak of it. It can conjure negative thoughts of a dimension void of activity, like dying for eternity with nothing to do (this image haunted me as a child).

But 'emptiness' is not 'nothingness'.

From a Buddhist perspective, 'emptiness' is alive and pregnant with possibility.

Imagine a house stripped of all furniture, fixtures and fittings. From one point of view, it is a cold place of nothingness devoid of the bustling energy of a family. From another point of view, it is a wonderful space of potential; an embryonic home waiting to evolve through lives, events and stories, as yet, unrealised. 'Emptiness' is the blank canvas of life, and it is a gift, not a curse.

Zen meditation – sitting still doing nothing

Zen meditation is famous for its monks who sit for hours

on end staring at a blank wall. This is the Zen Buddhist meditation practice of Zazen.

While the muddy-jar meditation technique uses a point of focus to engage and therefore quiet the mind, the practice of Zazen uses no such anchor. Instead, it simply observes whatever is happening in the mind at any given point without using a tool. In a way, someone practising Zazen, rather than watching the mud in the jar, becomes the mud in the jar. Given time, the mud will settle if left alone, irrespective of technique or anchor: so too our minds.

Some people prefer to use anchors to meditate while others do not. Personally, I practise Zazen. As someone who is goal-driven and slightly controlling, the instruction for focused-based meditation becomes something else I have to achieve and another thing added to my 'to-do' list. Zazen, sitting still doing nothing, frees me from this.

Both types of technique are excellent and both work. I have added the second because it would have been disingenuous of me to teach the more common focus-based meditation and not my personal practice.

Here are the instructions:

1. Sit down comfortably in your quiet place, don't slouch, keep your back straight.
2. Set a timer for whatever time you prefer – 5, 10, 15, 20 minutes. I use an incense stick which takes exactly 45 minutes to burn, but a timer is just as good.

3. Sit still, do nothing and just 'observe' what happens in your mind.

4. Sit still, do nothing and just 'observe' what happens in your mind.

5. Sit still, do nothing and just 'observe' what happens in your mind.

6. Sit still, do nothing and just 'observe' what happens in your mind.

7. Sit still, do nothing and just 'observe' what happens in your mind.

8. Sit still, do nothing and just 'observe' what happens in your mind.

9. Sit still, do nothing and just 'observe' what happens in your mind.

10. Time's up!

Over time, once thoughts are allowed to settle and return to wherever it is they are manufactured, you will be left with a glimpse of that ultimate power source the Buddhists call 'emptiness'. The more you glimpse it, the more you trust in both its existence and its potential to guide and help you in your life.

The postman always rings twice

As I was writing this chapter, the postman interrupted my flow with a knock at the door. I think my disgruntled look may have told him that he'd disturbed me but he kept talking nevertheless.

'What are you writing?' he asked, and keen not to appear rude, just focused, I told him how I was trying to explain the inexplicable with my 'unpeeling' analogy and the Zazen instruction.

'Gosh,' he said. 'it sounds like you are trying to explain God.' I hadn't thought about this before, but, you know what, he's got a good point.

Cheree Strydom, our South African singer-songwriter from Chapter 5, echoes the thoughts of the postman.

When talking about music, it's impossible for Cheree to hide the love, passion and excitement in her voice. Her enthusiasm is not only infectious but also has a depth and quality that feels other-worldly. I asked her if she felt that her music was in some way a spiritual experience.

'You couldn't have said it better! Music is God to me, if that makes sense?' I told her it most certainly did. 'It takes me to into a euphoric [state], and also makes me feel, somehow, even more connected to what I believe in.

'I can't pinpoint it, but just label it God. But it's my form of a god, different from the one we worship in a church or a specific person.'

Cheree, through her music, accesses life's essence in much the same way that Buddhists do through their meditation techniques, and Cal Newport does with his 'deep work'.

As I left the postman and returned to my office to complete this chapter, I turned on the light. It occurred to me that although I cannot see the electricity that powers the light on my writing desk, its existence, because of its effect on my life, is undeniable. It doesn't matter what name we give to this 'ultimate power source', we know that something propels our lives. Even the most cynical among us, who take a mechanistic view of life on earth, cannot deny that it is powered by something!

What is more important is how we use this source to improve our lives.

Holding the world up with your fingertips

At the beginning of this chapter, I spoke of the unbreakable relationship between this lesson, number 5, and the previous one, and how one facilitates the other.

I have already mentioned that your liver performs over five hundred functions, but there is other natural magic happening in your body all the time: your kidneys are currently cleaning your blood of toxins and in 24 hours will have filtered almost 200 litres of fluid; your heart is busy beating around 100,000 beats per day so that it can send 7,000 litres of blood through the estimated 60,000 miles of blood vessels feeding your organs and tissues. All this is happening without you knowing; your only proof is that you are alive.

Consider these processes. The glimpse of 'emptiness' that you will achieve via meditation is the source of all these wonderful phenomena. Develop trust in the knowledge that, if it can handle your liver, kidney and heart functions, it can also handle moving you towards a life of profitable work of your choice. You are not required to 'hold the world up with your fingertips' – it is spinning quite nicely on its axis without any of your assistance. All that is required of you is to choose what you want and then let the universe take care of the rest (if it needs help, it will send you teachers and instructions as we discussed in Lesson 3).

When you practise meditation, not only do you practise letting your thoughts subside, you in turn reveal your 'life source'. With each meditation session, you are building a bond with this inherent strength that will be supplying your dreams. It becomes an ally that, in time, you learn to trust wholeheartedly.

It is nevertheless undeniable that, for some, past disappointments, broken dreams and unfulfilled expectations have eroded the belief that it is possible to be 'anything you dream'. In all likelihood it is this lack of faith that has led to so many people becoming stuck in careers and jobs that they would leave in a heartbeat given the chance. To deny our past failures would be a mistake and to do so would make this book no more than a saccharine Pollyanna-like self-help guide.

I am not going to deny that the road to success can be troublesome at times. I am not going to say that this benevolent life will always keep us safe from harm and provide our lofty goals without cost. I am going to suggest we do what the Buddhists do when trouble arises: stare it right in the eye and find a way to the other side, regardless.

Lesson 6:
When things go wrong –
the law of karma

After walking the 88 Temple Pilgrimage, life-af-firming as it most certainly was, I still had some unanswered questions. One in particular concerned failure.

I remember that it was a beautifully crisp, sunny February morning and very cold. With still nearly a 1,000 kilometres left to walk, I had more pressing issues on my mind than this fleeting worry. But the uneasiness wouldn't leave me, and I couldn't fathom a suitable answer or solution. It's a situation familiar to most of us, and this next lesson is designed for those moments of doubt and disappointment that you will inevitably encounter in your search for purpose and prosperity.

By now, you know that this book is based on the premise that inherent in our desires and choices are the seeds of their success. Rather than asking you blindly to believe what I say, I have attempted to demonstrate the points through the framework of Buddhism, given its position at the fulcrum of religion, philosophy and science. I am aware of the limits of frameworks of thought and words (none of us, as yet, have all the answers). While I have direct and hard-earned experience of 'ask and it is given', there is an irrefutable problem – an elephant, in the room.

For every success story demonstrating my point, there is another totally disproving it. It has vexed me for years. How could this be, despite my positive experiences?

If we agree with the logic of the Buddhist teachings on 'emptiness' and 'dependent origination' (everything being connected), as described in the previous chapter, then nothing should be able to sit outside of the idea that all successes are possible.

Let's recap these teachings with a thought experiment.

Begin with a blank sheet of paper.

Draw a circle in the middle of the sheet. This represents the 'whole'.

By definition, everything is included in the 'whole'. Nothing can be separate from that which is whole and total.

Now, draw a straight perpendicular line outside of the circle. This is what I did when I was first told that nothing could exist outside of the 'whole'. The line represents separation; something separate from the 'whole'. I had demonstrated that existence can operate outside of totality. I had essentially debunked a major pillar of Buddhism.

Or so I thought.

My teacher smiled at my effort and shook his head. 'This,' he said pointing to the sheet of paper rather than the diagrams, 'is the whole'.

But I wasn't finished. I drew a new line, not on the paper, but on the table on which the paper rested. Raised eyebrows and a slightly smug grin challenged him again.

'Stand up,' he ordered. I stood and he showed me that the table on which I'd drawn the line now held the 'whole'.

I realised, then and there, that this could go on into infinity, just as space does with all its stars, planets and galaxies. Nothing can exist outside of the 'whole'. We really are 'all one'.

Within this 'all oneness', therefore, is every possibility that ever was, is or will be. Nothing can stand outside of this, so it must be true.

Following this thought experiment we arrive at the conclusion that, theoretically at least, anything is possible. Teachers have been telling us this for generations.

But then – and this was the crux of the worry that wouldn't leave me – why do people fail? Why do bad things happen to good people? Why do people die young? Why can't I conjure a tree out of the ether with thought alone when the theory suggests I ought to be able to do so? Despite my personal experience, this worry was the flaw in the theory.

And then it hit me. The answers were closer than I thought. In fact, the answers lay in a teaching that I already knew, but hadn't researched deeply enough.

Be careful what you ask for

The above thought experiment suggests our foundation is a source that contains the potential for all things. That same source, however, contains things we don't like as much as the things we covet: up *and* down, good *and* bad, success *and* failure.

The source of all things does not care whether you ask for good things or bad things to come into your life. Its job is simply to create.

If we believe this major teaching of Buddhism, we must concede that we are responsible for everything that manifests in our lives – at some level. Somewhere, somehow, we have chosen it into being. The answer regarding failure had eluded me for so long because I refused to accept it.

Even typing the following examples makes me both angry and sad. Eighteen months ago, a family friend died of cancer. She was just 38 and left behind a devastated husband and four beautiful children. My wife has always wanted to have children but cannot conceive, while others around her, some of whom don't want children particularly, fall pregnant seemingly at the drop of a hat.

Sitting next to a magnificent African elephant lying on the ground with a glassy stare and blood trickling down from the bullethole in its head is a trophy hunter looking proud of his day's achievement.

Does Buddhism want me to believe that the sufferers in all these stories asked for what has happened to them? Yes. That's precisely what it is saying.

Yet this teaching is not as brutal and uncompassionate as it initially seems. In fact, it offers some hope. We just have to learn to see through a slightly different lens to benefit from this lesson.

The white noise playing in many of our backgrounds, perhaps as a product of our vaguely religious school education, is a belief in a punitive God. This is what causes the resistance (it is certainly what was causing mine), when a teaching suggests that the bad things in our lives are our responsibility. Through the lens of a punitive creator, we interpret responsibility to mean fault and see the outcome as punishment. Who in their right mind wants to believe in these types of ideas? But this is not the teaching or belief of Buddhists.

Buddhism doesn't have a single creator at its helm, dishing out good things to good people and bad things to those tumbling from grace.* Instead, Buddhism believes in cause and effect, which they call 'karma'. No doubt you will have heard of karma – it's one of those Eastern terms that has permeated our Western lives.

The Sanskrit word karma translates as 'action', and means simply observable cause and effect. If I am nice

---

* Buddhism does have gods, but they are mere manifestations from the 'ultimate source' rather than punitive creators.

to you, you will probably be nice back. If I fail to show passion in my work, I'll most likely make a half-hearted effort and end up sacked. If I don't water a plant, it dies and I lose the potential shade of an oak tree. Karma is a natural law, no more punitive than gravity. For example, gravity doesn't punish whatever goes up by bringing it crashing to the floor. It is just 'being gravity'.

Please read the following instructions and then do the thought exercise:

Close your eyes and pay attention to what you are feeling right now. How does that feeling manifest in your body? Is there a little tension you didn't know you had? Where is it if there is? In which part of the body? If you can't feel anything, good or bad, what can you feel? Is there a blankness?

The point is that most of us, at any given time, are too busy to notice what feelings, thoughts and subtle emotions are operating as our default settings.

Now do this second exercise: Think of something that you really want to achieve. Close your eyes and notice the feelings that come up. Were they hopeful or fearful? Positive or doubtful? Did your mind start telling you all the reasons it won't happen?

Most of us are not aware of what feelings are coursing through our veins through the day. We drown them out by turning on the radio in the car, checking our social-media newsfeed, buying another coffee and so on. But it's important to pay attention; our feelings drive our thoughts. If your underlying feelings are negative, so will be your thoughts. Your negative thoughts and feelings will drive your decisions, actions and output. Your output will become your outcome delivered by the law of cause and effect, the law of karma.

Still don't want to believe me? I can appreciate the resistance to responsibility. Think of a day you woke up feeling grumpy. Now play the rest of the day out in your memory. You know as well as I do that unless you did something really drastic to improve your mood, the day was not a good one. Mood, mindset and outcome were news 30 years ago; today the connection is well documented and undeniable.

Our default beliefs ('I'm a failure – my dad told me so'; 'I'm really lucky, my mum always said I had nine lives') drive our feelings and thoughts. If we don't pay attention, we don't know what we are projecting onto the world.*

Blindness and inattentiveness to the feelings and thoughts providing the backdrop to our lives have a major impact on our day-to-day experiences. We should, literally, mind what we think, because it is our thoughts that shape our karma and, in turn, our lives.

There is another Buddhist teaching, inextricably linked with the idea of karma, which I am bound to

---

* An important note: ideas similar to karma can be found within secular, non-Buddhist maxims such as: 'You reap what you sow'; 'You make your own luck'; 'What goes around, comes around'; 'The more I practise, the luckier I get.'

mention while searching for a possible explanation of why bad things happen in our lives: reincarnation.

Reincarnation – Buddhist nonsense at its best?

Gary Chamberlain is a man who doesn't mince his words. After a 31-year career serving on the front line of the fire service and a 46-year 'hobby' participating in full-contact karate, he is a hard man in every sense of the word.

'I'm a pragmatist,' says Gary. 'You have to dry your eyes and not feel sorry for yourself. Deal with it, take action. Form a plan. Sitting on your hands, sucking your thumb and feeling sorry for yourself does absolutely nothing.'

It was a social-media post of Gary's titled, 'Why do bad things happen to good people?' that made me reach out for an interview. He turned out to be one of the most interesting people I have had the pleasure of meeting.

Gary had written the post with reference to a fire service colleague who is courageous, gregarious, positive and 'just a good guy!' All the indicators suggest that this is a man whose default setting is positive.

'This is a bloke who was on his way to a course when he saw a road traffic accident,' Gary explains. 'Out of the goodness of his heart, he stopped, gave assistance and got hit by a truck! Broke his back. He's been in pain ever since.'

Why does a man with the qualities of what Buddhists

call a Bodhisattva* and a generally positive attitude and state of mind manage to attract bad things into his life? Is it simply the harsh reality of pot luck? This lack of control over our fate for those who believe in a universe governed by chance, is a depressing thought, but Buddhism has another, more hopeful explanation. Namely, that within the 'whole' that we described earlier, nothing dies (where would it go after all?), it merely changes.

Let's use another thought experiment to investigate this idea further.

Imagine a tree full of summer leaves. During autumn, the leaves begin to wither, brown and fall. In essence, the leaves are dead. But are they? While they have changed form, they are still a big player in the ecosystem of life.

The decomposing leaves provide essential nutrients for the growth of new organisms and are part of the cyclical process maintaining all life on earth. So, in death the leaf provides life. It could be said that the leaf is reborn in the organism.

Many schools of Buddhism believe in reincarnation, and it was this doctrine, as well as the concept of

---

* In Mahayana Buddhism, a Bodhisattva is someone who delays reaching their own nirvana in order to show compassion to those still suffering in life. Simply, it points to qualities in those who provide service, compassion, courage and a desire to help others, despite the risks and loss to themselves. (It could reasonably be argued that all our wonderful staff in the emergency services are Bodhisattvas.)

karma, that initially prevented my full engagement with Buddhist teachings. However, as time went on, I began to see 'reincarnation' all around me and began to understand the value of the teaching. I had made a fundamental error in assuming that, as a novice to the teachings, I had fully grasped the concepts; much like novice martial-arts students who turn up to class on day one expecting to look, sound and feel like a Bruce Lee film. They are always shocked when the training makes them ache, the punches don't 'thwap' and they move like a newborn giraffe rather than with the stuntman-style grace of Jackie Chan!

I had made the same schoolboy error with my stereotypical thinking about reincarnation. In my limited view, I had thought it meant that Uncle Jack, run over by a dustcart, would come back as a zombie dog to terrorise his killers every Wednesday on bin collection day. It was a naïve and thoughtless interpretation of one of Buddhism's key ideas, which I couldn't buy into – so I rejected the idea out of hand.

But when I viewed reincarnation from the more practical and nuanced leaves-into-mulch-into-food-for-organisms perspective (as Buddhists would be more inclined to do), it made more sense. In fact, from this point of view, I could see life, death and reincarnation (rebirth), all around me: in the changing of the seasons, the cellular turnover of the body, even in the crimes, jail time and rehabilitation of convicted felons.

Another way that Buddhists like to describe

reincarnation is through the analogy of the relationship between a wave and the ocean. The ocean is seen as the 'whole', while the waves are the individual 'crests of life' that are born from it and recede once spent in an endless cycle of deathless water. Maybe a name change, from reincarnation to recycling, recreating or repurposing, might be more helpful.

When we combine both the ideas of karma (cause and effect) and reincarnation (nothing ever truly dies), a whole new level of understanding about our lives and universe opens to us. We draw closer to a possible explanation of why bad things sometimes happen to good people (and vice versa). Let's return to Gary's fireman friend who, despite being a fountain of goodness, had more than his fair share of bad luck, to see how these ideas *might* explain his poor fortune.

According to Buddhist teachings, it could be suggested that his current difficulties are the ripening effects of past negative actions/thoughts left over from *yesterday* (or earlier), and that his positive attitude *today*, despite his current hardship, will pay positive dividends *tomorrow* (or later). Of course, this is conjecture and it will do little to endear some people to the concepts of karma and rein- carnation, but the ideas are worth considering if only to make a stab at a possible theory of why good things happen to bad people. The alternative, when it comes to why bad things happen, is to believe either in the fates dished out by the punitive gods of various religions or in the arbitrariness of 'chance' suggested by science. For me, toeing the middle line of Buddhism fits my needs.

At first glance it appears that the idea of karma leaves us in a pretty hopeless situation; are we all bound to live out the consequences of past mistakes, from God knows how far back? But while we can't escape this 'karmic debt', once paid, it is over and our future life will be shaped by the lessons that we have learned from the experience. Of course, you must choose to look for the lessons inherent in difficulty.

Silver linings

Whether you choose to accept or not the ideas of karma and reincarnation to explain why bad things happen, doesn't change the fact that bad things do happen. However, whether or not we believe they come to pass is less important than what we choose to do when faced with such adversity.

Many of our bad moments are made worse by both fretting about them and resisting them. Take the intense physical pain of a migraine headache as an example. Although the pain, precipitated by whatever mistake we may have previously made (consuming too much chocolate, coffee or red wine, stress, too much or too little exercise or whatever), is undeniable, our relationship to it makes it either easier or more difficult to bear.

Jon Kabat-Zinn is the founder of MBSR, an

eight-week intensive Mindfulness-Based Stress Reduction programme, which is taught at his stress reduction clinic at the University of Massachussetts Medical Centre. Since the programme's inception in 1979, he and his staff have helped thousands of patients learn how to deal with chronic pain using the Buddhist tools of mindfulness meditation (although the course is secular in nature).

The programme provides strategies that help patients change their attitude to and relationship with their pain. It could be said that it helps them look for the 'silver linings' in their adversity.

One of Kabat-Zinn's methods of teaching people to deal with pain is the 'corpse exercise'. In this exercise, patients lie flat and still on the floor with their eyes closed.

Over the next 45 minutes, they are asked to direct their attention for a few brief moments to each part of the body, starting with the toes of the left foot and progressively working up and through the rest of the limbs and torso, culminating at the crown of the head. The instruction is simply to *observe* the sensation of each body part (pleasant, unpleasant or neutral) without any attempts to fix or change anything. In this way, they become the 'watcher' of pain rather than the 'victim'.

(Think back to the chapter on meditation. The primary skill developed in the Zazen technique of meditation is to observe objectively whatever is going on in the mind without undue attachment. You can do the same with pain.)

Pain, whether it be physical, mental, emotional or

even spiritual, is not our enemy, suggests Kabat-Zinn. It is simply the alarm system of our body warning us that something is wrong and requires attention. The trouble is that we are being encouraged to ignore the warnings and avoid the pain. According to one leading online market research company, the global topical pain relief market was valued at $7,481 million in 2017, and is projected to reach $13,276 million by 2025. That is a lot of over-the-counter pain relief.

Ironically, it is our dislike, fear and resistance to pain that keeps us chained to it. By putting our attention and effort into denying it, not only does it become more prevalent in our mind, it may also be exacerbated as our 'ignored' alarm system screams louder to be heard. If we don't listen to our pain, we will be unable to avoid the harm from which it may be attempting to protect us. In the corpse exercise of the MBSR programme, patients begin to see their pain not as an enemy but as an indicator of something being out of balance; and, more often than not, once the pain is embraced, and the lesson learned, it eases of its own non-opioid accord.

Next time you suffer any type of pain, take a moment to notice the 'add-ons' you create for yourself aside from the pain itself. For example, I am so resistant and fearful of migraine pain that I tense my jaw and shoulders against it, thus resulting in more pain. The Buddhists poetically call this vicious cycle of suffering caused by resistance, *samsara*. The opposite is *nirvana*. The way out of suffering, they say, is not to resist it but simply to 'observe it mindfully'. In this way, although the pain is indisputable, we cease fighting against it, and it is left alone to 'do its thing'. For me this results in a headache that lasts hours rather than days. A welcome relief indeed.

It's time to meet one of our Buddhist Millionaires for whom pain and difficulty are a daily occurrence.

Mo

He's known as Mo, but his real name is Moatez Jomni, and he's a 30-year-old British Paralympian athlete.

Tunisian-born Mo was left wheelchair-bound when, aged four, he was run over twice in quick succession.

'It was a hit and run. I was just four when it happened, just a kid. I can remember vividly, I was playing football in the street and sat down to rest on the pavement, and all of a sudden, this huge lorry comes and runs over my legs.

'I was lying in the road and then a taxi that was driving close behind the lorry ran over me too. Maybe the lorry was blocking the taxi's view.'

'After that, my life changed completely,' Mo told me.

Living in a very poor part of Tunisia, Mo's family could not afford a wheelchair for him; once he finally came out of the coma his friends and family used to carry him on their backs to school. Seeing no long-term future in Tunisia, Mo's parents worked slavishly to secure asylum in the UK, his adopted home.

For many para-athletes, Olympians or otherwise, the limits of their disability within their chosen sporting field is just one mountain to climb; there are other, often more serious, challenges. For wheelchair-bound athletes, problems with blood circulation, the complications of postural distortion and constant pain.

'From age 21 to 22, I was the sickest person ever. I had a fall and spent two years, on and off, in hospital. It affected my injury, and I had pressure sores, and it affected my spinal cord… you're a slow healer when you're disabled,' explained Mo.

'At that point, I was wondering, what the hell am I going to do with my life? Things were really bad.'

During his young life, Mo had suffered more than his fair share of hardship and you could have forgiven him if he had wanted to retreat into a shell of bitterness. But no, not Mo.

'One day, I was about 23, I sat down and said to myself, "This can't be your life." In that instant something clicked.' Mo told me.

In a moment of inspiration, he decided to refocus on an aspiration he had had when he was sixteen, a goal that his naturally concerned parents discouraged, but which now, as a man not a teenager, he had the autonomy to pursue. Mo was going to be an athlete.

Mo contacted UK Athletics, who put him in touch with the Weir Archer Academy. Jenny Archer, coach of the legendary multiple Paralympic medalist David Weir, assessed Mo's potential and agreed to help him 'give it a go'.

This is a list of Mo Jomni's achievements to date:

- Paralympic finals, Rio de Janeiro, 2016
- IPC Athletics World Championships bronze medal, Doha, 2015, 200m T53 (race classification)
- IPC European Championships:
  Gold medal, Swansea, 2014, 400m T53
  Bronze medal, Swansea, 2014, 800m T53
  Gold medal, Grosseto, 2016, 200m T53
  Silver medal, Grosseto, 2016, 400m T53
  Silver medal, Grosseto, 2016, 800m T53
  Bronze medal, Grosseto, 2016, 100m T53

Mo is still pushing hard and is aiming higher and higher in his career. He was leaving the interview with me to fly to yet another European Championships event (he won medals again, twice).

I was reticent about asking him if he considered that the accident in his youth was somehow a 'blessing in disguise' – the question sounded unintentionally corny in my head having heard his story. I was relieved when he said it was.

'I believe in that. What I went through is like a lesson. Don't waste your life, life is too short,' said Mo. 'I think you have to go through a very lengthy process to create something of yourself. At the end of the day, my favourite creature would be a phoenix. It's better to be born out of your own destruction than to actually hold it.'

Mo had hit the nail on the head, certainly from a Buddhist perspective. We cannot change the fact that bad things happen to both good, and not-so-good people. Whether or not we accept the Buddhist doctrines of karma and reincarnation is irrelevant. However, no matter how it arises, we can meet the adversity in just two ways: with resistance or acceptance. As author Neale Donald Walsch counsels in his book, *Conversations with God*, 'Whatever we resist, persists; what we look into, fades away.'

Expect the unexpected

For you, as a potential Buddhist Millionaire, there will undoubtedly come a time on your journey when things don't go your way.

If you can accept the inevitability of this from the very first step, then you will lessen the pain considerably; much in the same way that committing to a full-contact tackle in rugby hurts far less than tentatively reaching out and hoping for the best, which almost always results in fingers bent back and a sore shoulder.

As well as steeling yourself against the bad times, you can also practise, as Mo says, 'not holding your own destruction'. You can choose to let it go.

Using the practice of meditation, you can choose to become the observer of your difficulties rather than a panicking participant. If you are suffering adversity, when you sit for your meditation session, make the problem the object of your focus rather than the mud.

Bring the problem to mind: where does it reside? Where do you feel it in your body? Just observe. If it were a colour, what would it be? Just observe. Is it hot or cold? Just observe. Be with the problem, watching from the wings with curiosity rather than judgement.

While the difficulties will still have to be experienced and lived through, with practice you will stop adding further trauma and prolonging them for longer than necessary. You will have moved from a position of *samsara*, with all its grasping, fighting and resisting, to *nirvana,* with its characteristics of ease, acceptance and effortlessness.

In this new state of calm, even in the face of pain, it is possible to see the silver lining, and the hidden lesson, that is inherent in every cloud, should we pay enough attention to notice.

Lesson 7:
Invisible currencies

Traditionally, Japanese massage therapists were blind. It is said that without the use of sight they were better able to tune into the energy of their patients and feel where the source of discomfort predominated. The problem for many of us is that we rely far too much on what we can see, unlike the Japanese masseurs of old.

The scientific method of 'proof' is vital for our education, growth and evolution. No one wants to commit to theories and ideas that turn out to be, at best, worthless, and at worst, detrimental to our lives. But I would argue that we all place far too much reliance on both the findings and evidence of others, including scientists. We have given up responsibility for discovering things for ourselves, so easy is it to google information and find others' research, video tutorials and online lessons.

Please don't misunderstand me. I am not suggesting that we all wander through life in a naïve fog, rejecting evidence that doesn't happen to fit the beliefs we may hold on any given day: not at all. If I'm in need of emergency care, certainly, I would prefer a doctor to an aromatherapist. What I am suggesting is that there is often more to life than meets the eye, including the eyes of those wielding the scientific method.

Not everything of value can be seen. There are also what I call invisible currencies.

Money panic!

Sunni Jardine, our rugby-playing Buddhist Millionaire from Part I, texted me in a panic.

'Dad, I think I've got myself into a bit of trouble.' These are not the words that any parent wants to read.

Sunni had reached the entrance gates to Birmingham station, for the 10.19am train to Coventry, only to discover that there wasn't enough money on his card to pay the fare. Now running late for rugby training, he checked with his bank: it was true. He had no money (actually he had 54 pence).

To all intents and purposes, Sunni was, at that moment, cash poor. Yet he still qualifies as a Buddhist Millionaire – albeit a fledgling.

When you make the leap and decide finally to go after your dream work, whether that be a coveted position, job role or starting your own business, unsurprisingly, you will have money worries; indeed it is probably partly the fear of lack of money that has kept you stuck in a less than ideal work environment. Right? This is natural, normal and something every Buddhist Millionaire must work through.

It is likely that you have dependents, as well as pressing financial obligations: this can be a problem for many starting out on a new path.

As GB Olympic basketball captain Drew Sullivan told us back in Chapter 7: 'For a lot of people in a relationship, there tends to be the worry of taking care of their partner or their kids, but it can also lead to resentment if you don't follow your dreams.

'Your first responsibility with happiness is to yourself.'

It is obviously easier to make the transition if both you and your dependants trust that your bold move towards dream work is going to work out just fine. Ideally, you could show them evidence that everything will move in the right direction. And I would argue that you can – it's just that they will have to wear different spectacles to see it.

£1 million now, or £1,000 a week for the rest of your life?

I couldn't be happier that Sunni has decided to chase a life that most don't dare dream of or imagine they could attain – that of a professional sportsman. I'm equally delighted that he has run out of money.

It is easy, almost unavoidable, to fall into the trap of

seeing money the primary indicator of your success. This isn't to say that money isn't essential for modern living; a key premise of this book is the acceptance of money's importance. I stand by my claim that it is possible to create work that is both meaningful and profitable and I have no intention of reneging on that idea in favour of a more 'it's okay to be broke but happy' premise.

But when we look at the world through lenses that enable us to see only money as a measure of success, then we are blind to other achievements which, although not fiscal, are equally important. It is one key aspect of the epidemic of modernity: to value only that which can be purchased, another one being the desire for instant gratification.

In 2018, *Guardian* columnist, Hannah Jane Parkinson wrote a fascinating article titled 'Would you take £1m now, or £1,000 a week for the rest of your life?'[9]

She reported the story of a Canadian teenager who not only won the lottery jackpot the first time she played, but was faced with the dilemma outlined in the headline. She ended delaying gratification and opting for the instalments rather than the lump sum (although £1,000 a week is hardly a paltry sum).

The most interesting parts of the article were some facts about lottery winners and their neighbours in general. Not only does evidence show that lottery winners in America are more likely than the average person to declare bankruptcy within three to five years, but also

that their neighbours frequently end up in financial difficulty as well.

Why on earth would that be? It's simple: it's likely that
both the lottery winners and their neighbours are looking
at the world wearing 'money spectacles'. The things that
the money can buy give the lottery winners importance
(albeit superficial), while the neighbours, fearing they may
be left behind, try to keep up using lines of credit. This is
what happens when money is deemed the only currency
of success. You end up giving it too much importance and
chasing it into trouble.

When, for whatever reason, your bank account
bottoms out, you are forced to look elsewhere for value.
And this is where you'll find invisible currencies.

London-Birmingham-Coventry

If you are going to pursue a career in professional sports, if
you can tolerate the bumps, bruises, concussion, gruelling
exercise schedules and ridiculous amounts of strength and
conditioning training involved, I would suggest rugby!

Rugby, has been described as 'a ruffian's game played
by gentlemen', while football is said to be 'a gentlemen's
game played by ruffians'. I have no opinion either way,
but what I do like about professional rugby clubs is that
their players are as tough as nails, and well educated to
boot.

Rugby clubs encourage their young players not only

to do their utmost to master the professional skills of the sport, but also to finish their education at the same time. With this in mind, they offer the likes of young men like Sunni a place on an 'academy programme'.

In a nutshell, the academy programme allows young, aspiring rugby players to play professionally while simultaneously completing university degrees. The players train with top athletes but compete in the slightly less demanding A, B and C teams, enabling them to manage, just about, the demands of professional sport and university education.

It is a system unique to rugby, as far as I can tell. Other sports – football for example – favour an 'all or nothing' approach where young players sacrifice everything to dive headlong into professional training in the hope that they will one day be selected for a top-tier team. Few make it. Many are dropped unceremoniously by the wayside, with their dreams of life as a football superstar left tattered, and no further education to fall back on.

This contrast in development style sport is indicative of soccer's short-term thinking. Rugby values 'the invisible currency' of education, preferring to nurture professional talent over a period of years; soccer, aiming for and selling its young players the dream of football stardom, offers a high-risk, high-returns bet that some will win and many won't.

But this is not why I chose this example. I chose it because it was the wonderful, admirable long-term strategy of the rugby academy system that caused Sunni to run out of money!

In a normal week, Sunni lives out of three homes. He lives on Birmingham University campus four days a week, in Coventry in shared accommodation with other young rugby academy players for two days a week and, if he has the energy, he returns to our home in London for a night a week. It was the underestimated cost of the triad of train commutes that had rendered Sunni almost penniless.

Clearly, the 'Bank of Dad' was going to help out, but I was also pleased that it provided me with an opportunity to give some long-overdue financial advice and also to shine a light on the idea of invisible currencies.

It is vital to embrace this chapter's lesson if you are going make it over the hump of an emptying (or empty) bank balance. Many of you may be deciding to leave work that, although possibly no longer inspiring, at least affords a standard of living to which you have become accustomed. If the value of leaving your career comfort zone doesn't equal or exceed the value of you staying put, then it will be very difficult to find the motivation to continue through the hardship.

So, what are invisible currencies exactly? They are things that hold value but currently cannot be exchanged for pounds and pence (or any other fiscal currency for that matter).

Let's continue with the example of Sunni's situation. On paper, his bank account shows the same degree of health as one of his friend's, whom we'll call Geoff. Geoff is a nice lad, but hasn't yet found his mark in life. Since leaving college (which he failed to complete), he has lived on his parents' couch playing video games – and this is no exaggeration. As far as money goes, Sunni and Geoff are in the same boat, despite the efforts Sunni is making to manage a degree and a burgeoning rugby career. It's a fact that bothers Sunni immensely.

From my perspective as a parent, if Geoff had asked me to help him out of his 'no money' situation, I would have offered little more than a pile of application forms for job interviews. When Sunni needed help, because of the evidence of his invisible currencies, I felt it appropriate to help financially. But this is not about me and my parenting choices…

Let's identify some of the invisible currencies in Sunni's life:

- Rugby skill development
- Strength, fitness and coordination development
- Time management skills developed through having to be in different places at different times
- Discipline, self-control and self-restraint (resisting normal 19-year-old behaviour in favour of training *and* study)
- Written communication and other academic skills developed through studying for a degree.

Let's take a look at another example (so as not to overdo my 'proud dad' stories) of where invisible currencies might also be found.

The vicious circle of inexperience

Leaving school or university to enter the world of work, or even transitioning from one work sector, where you have experience, to another where you have none, can teach you a great deal about invisible currencies.

When starting a new business venture or when applying for that first job as a newbie, the proverbial 'white belt', is at the bottom of the career ladder. With their current work experience and skills, they are often unable to realise their financial worth much above a basic salary, if indeed they can secure a position at all. I have often wondered at that cruel vicious circle where a young job applicant is rejected for a position owing to a lack of experience. Where, without that first job, will they begin to acquire such experience?

According to the most recent findings of a report from the UK Civil Society Almanac,[10] it is estimated that 11.9 million people undertake volunteer work at least once a month in the UK. Volunteering is one of the easiest and most obvious ways to develop a multitude of invisible currencies. The report goes on to list the following as some of 'the benefits of student volunteering':

- Giving back and helping others
- Developing skills and work experience
- Building a community
- Meeting new people

All of these are examples of invisible currencies earned from the wonderful work of volunteering. They are not directly exchangeable for money right now. However, they will undoubtedly contribute to the accrual of future great rewards, including financial recompense. Yet many people fail to grasp the worth of this unpaid labour with its delayed gratification.

I want it all, and I want it now

I would argue that most of the great things in life hold a value that isn't easily exchanged for money: a beautiful sunrise, the song of the skylark, giving someone a compliment, holding the door open for someone, letting a car into the lane ahead of you.

As a child of the 70s, I remember having to wait until the end of the week before my brother and I, 50 pence piece clutched firmly in hand, walked excitedly to the local shops to buy a paper bag of penny sweets. The true value was the invisible currency of patience fostered through a week-long wait.

I am not going to haul out that old-man cliché that 'things were different in my day' (they were!) – but it is undeniable that today we live in an age of instant gratification very different from yesteryear. We no longer have to spend time researching homework answers in the *Encyclopedia Britannica* We don't now spend weeks saving for something when the local supermarket will give us a 'third one free' when we buy two for next to nothing in the first place. Neither do we wait nervously for weeks on end for holiday snaps to be delivered, which may be what we expected, but equally turn out to be a pile of sepia-toned blurs, or worse, someone else's honeymoon shots – we have our own selfies to hand, instantly, on our phones!

While modern life has certainly improved in many ways, we seem to have lost, or at least diminished, our respect for things such as invisible currencies. It will be our reappreciation of them that will help us through the early and sometimes fiscally difficult stages of Buddhist Millionairedom. It's time, I suggest, to start looking for the value in the seemingly valueless.

Small wins

As I mentioned in the previous chapter, it is important to recognise the silver linings of storm clouds. Motivational speaker and author, Wayne Dyer, sums it up quite nicely when he says: 'To see change, change the way you see.'

Finding value that isn't obvious, or is of a different currency to that with which you are familiar, takes effort and practice. To get you started, I am going to teach you the 'small wins' exercise, one of my favourites borrowed from a schoolteacher friend. In order to build her pupils' confidence and feelings of self-worth, she encourages them to acknowledge their small wins with the use of a marble jar.

Each child has a marble jar on their desk. When they have done something notable (completed a task on time, put great effort into a piece of work, shown kindness to another pupil etc*), my friend performs 'the marble ceremony'.

With pomp and ceremony, she asks the child to come to the front of the class with their marble jar to receive a marble as their prize. The child unscrews the lid of the jar and drops in the marble with a clink and, after receiving applause, happily returns to their chair. After several weeks, once a pupil's marble jar is full of marbles, they receive a small prize.

The public ceremony, the supportive applause, satisfying clink of the marble and the visual enticement of a filling jar, are all positive experiences in the child's mind. The child quickly recognises that effort leads to more marbles ('small wins') and in this way begins to appreciate that invisible currencies (kindness, effort, politeness, etc) eventually become a tangible prize.

---

* Note that she looks to reward efforts rather results in line with the growth mindset philosophy as taught by Dr Carol Dweck in her book *Mindset*.

It is a wonderfully simple exercise that achieves results with children and one that can also benefit all of us on the path of the Buddhist Millionaire.

Allow me one more example from my days as a tennis coach. The majority of recreational tennis players booking a one-to-one lesson with a tennis pro want to improve their serve.

The serve in tennis begins the game. It is the superstar skill of tennis, in that it is the thing viewers admire most when they watch professionals play. It is the tennis equivalent of the one-punch knock-out in boxing, or a hole-in-one in golf. The trouble is, it's the most complex and difficult skill to master.

Not only does the serve require the coordination of a lot of complex movements, it must also hit the ball into the smallest target zone of the tennis court: the service box. Needless to say, a novice server experiences a lot of 'failures' before they succeed.

Very often, a tennis pro builds their reputation (and fills their teaching diaries) on the back of their ability to help players improve their serve: 'Wow, go to Matt, he really helped me with my first serve'; 'Man, did you see what Dave did for my topspin second serve? The guy's a genius.'

I became fascinated by the challenge of teaching the serve and committed myself to the guarantee that I could substantially improve any recreational player's serve in just half an hour. Needless to say, many came to see if it was true. And it was.

But I didn't do anything special. I didn't have any super-technical insights into the biomechanics of the service action; I didn't research the optimum load of the legs in relation to the upward thrust. I didn't calculate the best angle of impact or ideal speed of acceleration and deacceleration of the racket head through the ball. I did none of these (in fact my colleagues did these things much better than me). No, all I did was ask my students to change the spectacles through which they viewed success. I asked them to look, instead, for invisible currencies.

As I've mentioned, one of the biggest challenges in serving is that the area into which the ball must land to be considered a 'success' is significantly smaller than for all other shots. With a serve, if it lands outside of the service box, it is 'out', and you have 'failed'.

A novice, or even an intermediate server, while their technique is developing, is more likely to hit 'out' than 'in' and this can be extremely demotivating. Repeated failure is enough to crush anyone's spirit. But is a serve that goes 'out' really a failure?

Well, yes, and no – it depends on how you look at it. If the only measure of success is 'in' or 'out', then, yes, it is a 'failure'. But if you observe that, although you are not yet hitting the serve in the box, you are consistently contacting the ball (which you weren't before), you will see that you are improving. Taking this view, the heart lifts a little, the shoulders relax, and further progress is encouraged through a more enjoyable approach to learning.

It's the same when we are building profitable, meaningful work. If your only measure of success is money (the serve in the box), I'm sorry to say, you are going to 'fail' a lot more before you 'succeed'. If, however, you start looking for other markers of progress, the small wins and the invisible currencies, you will always win.

Again, I urge you not to misunderstand my point. I am in no way suggesting that you sugar-coat the challenges you'll find along the Buddhist Millionaire path. I'm not condoning that you pretend, head in sand, that the challenges don't exist, or that it's okay not to be where you want to be. You have a goal to reach, and you need to reach it, but it makes no sense falling off the path, demotivated, because you failed to notice the massive (albeit subtle) gains you have made so far.

I spoke to Selina Lamy about this, our Citibanker turned life coach from previous chapters, and this is what she said: 'I totally agree, you must look for other markers of success other than money (although it's important). There is so much other value in doing a job that I love, and how everybody benefits from that. I am much happier and fulfilled in myself, but also far more present for the boys because I don't come home carrying the burdens of a job which depletes me. I couldn't have predicted the non-financial gains of this change in direction, but they are huge and significant.'

Noticing invisible currencies

Try this exercise:

- On the far right of a piece of paper, write down a money goal linked to work. For example, you might write: 'To earn £5,000 a month selling my art.'
- Now, on the opposite side of the paper, write down where you are, from a money point of view, at the moment: 'I'm currently earning nothing at all and am £2,000 in debt after funding art materials with my credit card.'
- You now have both ends of your 'money spectrum'. You have honestly stated where you are, (with no denial) at one end and where you aim to be (with no weakening of goals or standards), at the other.
- Draw a line connecting the two poles.
- Then, in between, start filling in all the invisible currencies you have earned so far along the way, such as: 'more free time', 'less stress' etc.

Stick this chart on the wall or to the fridge and keep adding to it every time you earn a new invisible currency.

Also, from time to time, when your money situation changes, add that too. In this way, you will get into the habit of acknowledging and honouring invisible currencies, while simultaneously noting that they do indeed lead to money!

As you can see, this is just a more grown-up version of the marble jar exercise used to inspire the children. Feel free to use it instead. I do.

Lesson 8:
Love, gratitude and
the heart (sutra)

Japan is famous for its *sakura* – cherry blossom.

The subtly pink-tinged bloom is revered by the Japanese, and every year, they celebrate its appearance with *hanami* – literally, 'watching flower' – festivals. As the spring weather warms and the cherry trees explode into a mass of candyfloss-pink, friends, families and loved ones come together beneath them to eat, drink (often a *lot* of sake), laugh, catch up and revel in the beauty and poignancy of the transience of the *sakura*.

Sakura has long been held by Buddhists to be a symbol of the impermanence and ephemeral nature of life (*mujō*), since the blossoms usually last no longer than two days before they drop from their branches and collect below on a growing funeral pyre of pink and white.

While in Japan, I wrote about the *sakura* in my journal:

Fallen pink flower,
Lying in the rain,
Still beautiful
In its dying.

I almost didn't make a note of them. I almost didn't notice the cherry trees that had bloomed uncharacteristically early in the grounds of one of the temples of the 88 pilgrimage. And to miss that sight would have been both a massive mistake and a source of constant regret.

Corporate giants – the beasts without a heart?

If you cut Matt Hastings in half, you would likely find he was made of Buddhist Millionaire juice (if there were such a thing).

Matt was recommended to me as a Buddhist Millionaire candidate on the back of the referral, that he was 'different, really different; he's just what you're looking for'. Although not knowing what to expect, I wasn't disappointed.

I stood waiting in the car park of a Cornish park-and-ride as Matt pulled up in his old-school Aintree green Land Rover. With a cheery wave, he beckoned me into his car and we drove off to a beach side café to chat. I liked him immediately.

Matt is someone I have come to consider a 'corporate

maverick', partly due to a section of his Linkedin bio that reads: 'He set up his first start-up at 17 (A New Generation) and has been disrupting traditional businesses ever since.' Consequently, he is the perfect candidate to elucidate this eighth lesson.

Although he has a university degree (First class BSc (Hons) in Renewable Energy Technologies & Environmental Resource Management from Plymouth University), Matt takes pride in the fact that most of his knowledge and experience has been hard earned from that other well-known educational establishment: the University of Life. Armed with a vibrant spirit (he has the words 'Master your spirit' tattooed on his back, although he laughingly confesses that they read back to front, having been obtained during a less than sober holiday in Biarritz as a 19-year-old), Matt tells me he is 'obsessed with trying to do things a bit differently'.

'I think, from a spiritual perspective, I've always been fascinated by searching for self-honesty,' he explains. 'The only way I feel like I can grow as a person is by [regularly] checking in where my head is at.'

In 2001, following the Twin Towers tragedy of 9/11, much of the world's economy went into crisis and so too did Matt's media business, Havoc Marketing.

'The world just died,' he told me over lunch. All the money went out of media and advertising.

'Looking back, it came at a particular moment in my life when I thought, "I'm not enjoying London, I'm not enjoying my job. Money isn't everything. Something's got to change." So, he left the UK and headed for New Zealand, inspired by images of the country's stunning natural beauty.

'I lived in New Zealand for two years; learned how to surf, snowboard, fly-fish – the most spiritual sport of them all – and met my wife within four weeks of being out there,' he adds with a smile.

Matt and his new wife returned to the UK. Although originally from Scotland, his wife didn't want to return there and he, already burned out by the hustle and bustle of city life, didn't want to return to London, so they ended up in Plymouth.

'I landed on renewable energy in 2005. I thought, "That is the place where you get, hopefully, decent money and you feel good about what you're doing,"' he explained.

A cleaner, greener planet

That renewable energies are potentially big business is no longer news and where there is big business, there are corporate giants. One of those giants is Centrica Plc.

Centrica is a British multinational energy and services company. Its principal activity is supplying electricity and gas to businesses and domestic consumers in the UK, Ireland and North America. With an operating income of £1.392 billion in 2018, it more than sings to the giant's signature tune 'Fee-fi-fo-fum'. Very often these mammoth merchants with their heads high in the clouds of profit and loss fail to see what lies beneath them; neither the beautiful *sakura* blossom of the cherry tree nor indeed the 'spiritually guided' work ethics of corporate mavericks like Matt Hastings.

Matt admits that his mind and his business vision tend to operate a couple of years ahead of the 'regular curve'. When he joined Centrica in April 2014, with the sole objective of convincing the business to pursue a vision for local energy markets, the odds were very much stacked against him. One of the criticisms levelled at large corporations is that their profit obsession often blinds them to visionary strategies and ideas. But in 2016, Matt secured an unprecedented £19 million from Centrica to fund a trial of his vision – the UK's first local energy market in Cornwall.

'I think there is a fundamental shift going on, more so in some industries than others,' said Matt. 'We're certainly not [fully] there, but we're on the first steps of that journey where I think that corporates are gaining a sense of soul, they're starting to get a soul muscle.

'Whether you work in banking, energy, insurance, or whatever, they're starting to realise that, actually, unless you stand for something, what the hell's the point? If you want a business in the future, you have to do what's best for the people, not just what's best for your shareholders.'

The meaning of life

The 'deeper' meaning of life is always thrumming quietly in the background should you care to listen. Sometimes, though, you need someone or something to remind you that it is there. For Centrica, it was Matt Hastings, and for me, while on the 88 Temple Pilgrimage, it was Hajime San (Mr Beginnings whom you met earlier in the book).

I would have marched straight past the transient wonder of the early-blooming *sakura* had it not been for Hajime's words still ringing in my ears from our time spent together: 'Don't forget the heart of the pilgrimage, Matto San; don't forget the Heart Sutra.'

The *Hannya Shingyō* – Heart Sutra – is a central teaching in Buddhism and essential to the 88 Temple Pilgrimage. In this case 'Heart', means 'core of' rather than kindheartedness, but its lessons are said to develop 'good-hearted' qualities, nevertheless.

The aphoristic prayer of the Heart Sutra is chanted three times at each of the 88 temples. The purpose of its recitation is to awaken wisdom, compassion and kindness. I cannot say for certain that chanting about wisdom and compassion leads to the development of wisdom and compassion, but I can say that, as the pilgrimage wore on, and the chants stacked up, something in me became a little lighter and friendlier.

Every one of us – you, me, Matt Hastings, corporate giants, everyone – suspects that there is more to life than what is currently being expressed, yet it's easy to get side-tracked from our ideals. This may be the case for you also as you chase down your goal of becoming a Buddhist Millionaire. This chapter's lesson aims to remind you to look up from your goal, from time to time, so as not to miss the blossom.

Try this exercise for fun: Next time you are in your local high street either shopping, running errands or getting lunch, STOP! Now look up at the upper floors and rooftops of the buildings you have walked past a hundred times. Take a moment to see what you would have missed if you had continued blindly whizzing about your day. When I do this, I'm always stunned at what I didn't realise was right before my eyes, just an attentive head tilt away.

Moving on, let me ask you this question: is the underlying motivation of life good, bad or indifferent? Or to ask it another way: does life prefer to create, destroy or do nothing? I'll tell you why I ask: because the answer provides the basis for everything we do in our personal, professional and social lives.

It's a tricky one, isn't it? Bearing in mind that through history people have been successful in all three motivations. Who is right? If life's motivation is goodness, how can people, as they do, become so proficient at bad stuff? If, as some others suggest, life doesn't care either way, why should we care to better ourselves, and is it even possible?

This question has been on my mind, almost plaguing

me, since my teenage years. While this book doesn't aspire to answer the great 'meaning of life' question, I have some thoughts that may be relevant for you.

Ultimately, despite the bad things that happen (reread the chapter on karma to deal with this knotty conundrum) life is good. Furthermore, I would suggest that life is loving, and really wants us all to do well!

If life's motivation was anything other than good, loving and creative then, quite simply, none of us would be here. If life was a destroyer, or at least a 'not bovvered' type of teenage apathetic, it wouldn't have wielded the creative wand to power us into being. That very first amoeba, way back when, would have stayed unborn.

The fact that I have written this book and that you are taking the effort to read it (thank you very much), is testimony to the fact that life, actually, is one of the good guys and wants us to do well (or at least keep spreading our genes). It's good to know we have the big gun on our side, and that it has a couple more gifts that might accelerate our progress on the path of the Buddhist Millionaire.

Love and gratitude

So much has been written about love and gratitude (often in a way that makes me a little uneasy), that I was hesitant to focus on them here. But these two emotions are central to securing profitable, meaningful work, and it seems right to include them at this stage of the journey. What I will attempt, however, is to avoid clichés and saccharine advice.

Early on, we discussed that at any given time, all of us are either travelling towards a destination positively or away from one, negatively. While the end destination may be one and the same, the motivations to travel are worlds apart.

In his book, *Letting Go*, Dr David R. Hawkins, describes a scale of feelings and emotions ranging from negative to positive. These are: shame, guilt, apathy, grief, fear, desire, anger, pride, courage, neutrality, willingness, acceptance, reason, love, joy (and gratitude), and peace.

It will come as no surprise to see love and gratitude so far along the lighter scale of emotions. All of us have experience of how good it feels to help someone in a time of need. And when we feel good, and operate from a place of 'lighter state' emotion, life seems to run more smoothly. We don't need to get metaphysical about how and why this works; we just need to look at our own lives to know that it does.

I have a friend who prides himself on his scepticism, atheism and general resistance to any 'hoodwinkery' and 'tomfoolery' that may spout from the mouths of those extolling the virtues of love and gratitude. Yet even he cannot deny that his life tends to run more smoothly when he's in a kinder mood. He explains away the fortune and good luck that often follow those with a positive attitude as 'confirmation bias' – i.e. a product of simple neurological and biochemical processes performed by the brain to support information or beliefs that confirm our previously existing beliefs or biases. However it is explained, in metaphysical, poetic, religious or scientific terms, the truth remains that positive feelings and emotions are more useful to our cause than negative.

Counting your lucky stars

It takes effort and practice to make the habit of gratitude part of the patchwork of your life. It sounds ludicrous to suggest that being grateful needs to be developed, but, like all habits, it does.

The default mode of modern society is to blame, find fault and highlighting the frailties of any given situation. Take the broadcast news. The majority of reports have a negative undertone, with a token feel-good story left for a 90-second slot at the end to lighten the day. I'm not suggesting for one moment that Pollyanna should host all news bulletins from now on and only report on the good stuff in life, but that the balance, currently, is skewed towards negativity. Knowing this, it is up to us to develop the capacity for gratitude.

In your transition from where you are now to where you want to be, there will be challenging times; these are the perfect moments to develop gratitude, lighten your feelings and bring some emotional balance back into your life.

Try this simple exercise to ease you into the spirit of gratitude: on waking in the morning, before getting out of bed, lie still for a few moments. Think of one thing for which you are grateful. Remember our earlier lesson on working smart; you don't have to be sycophantically grateful for everything in your life – just pick something. For example, this morning I woke up and realised that, for the last seven nights, I haven't woken needing my asthma inhaler – great, thanks. Look for these sort of things: normal, real, everyday stuff. Finish the exercise, even if you have to force it, with a big smile. There's significant evidence to suggest that a 'mechanical' smile made in the absence of happiness quickly encourages happiness to follow, as if the brain is 'tricked' into managing the discrepancy. Try it. It works.

Once you have begun to develop the muscle of gratitude, not only are you better equipped to find more silver linings in storm clouds, but also to notice the wonderful, subtle gifts that life bestows endlessly upon you – should you care to notice.

This is going to help your transition into profitable, meaningful work in a number of ways.

Patience

When chasing any goal, there is always the issue of patience to contend with.

Let's say that you are reading this book and are

inspired to start moving towards your dream careers and away from the job that you are merely enduring simply to pay the bills.

All hyped up and ready to roll, you have worked through the preceding chapters and decided what it is you would really love to be. A rock star maybe? Great. A CEO? Nice. A stay-at-home parent with a cottage business? Lovely.

Your journey began with your decision, the most important part, but there is still a way to go from point A to point B. For the time being, you still have to survive a job you might grow to dislike intensely, not least because now you have somewhere you would rather be. This is when gratitude is a useful tool.

When leaving any relationship – and work is just one type – you can either do it kindly or unkindly. On Dr Hawkins' emotional scale, these ways are miles apart.

Unfortunately, I can speak from direct experience of both. In my younger, headstrong days, when I had decided to move on, I managed the transition with belligerence, impatience and, often, childishness. I'm not proud of this and wonder if, in my immaturity, I somehow needed mentally to dislike and push away my former life in order to move forward and recreate myself: metaphorically burning old bridges, in case I lost my nerve and tried to return. It was a tactic that, although unpleasant, worked until, with age, I realised it didn't have to be this way.

With experience, when the familiar yearnings for

change started to let me know it was time to evolve, I approached the move by looking back rather than forward.

I started to reflect on all the wonderful times and experiences that my current work environment had afforded me. I listed all I had learned, the ways in which I had grown and how being where I was now was preparing me for where I wanted to be. In this way, I felt a joyful continuum rather than an impatient and angry separation.

With this new attitude, with honesty, kindness and, of course, gratitude, I was able to approach those who needed to be told of my plans to move on with tact and respect. On several occasions, those I was leaving even helped me move in the direction of my new goals. It was a great change in attitude for me, fuelled by gratitude, and one that I sincerely recommend.

Metta – the art of loving kindness

Metta is a Sanskrit word that translates as 'loving kindness', 'goodwill', 'benevolence', 'friendliness' and 'compassion'. All pretty uplifting feelings and emotions.

The ultimate goal of Buddhism is to cultivate wisdom so that you can cultivate kindness towards others and help release them from suffering in all its guises. A pretty tough ask, I think you'll agree, and slightly outside the remit of this book; after all, I just want you to do work that you love and make money doing it! *Metta*, the art of loving kindness, is going to help you.

Think of five people you know who are imbued with the qualities of happiness, kindness and friendliness. Now think of five who regularly demonstrate the opposite, sourpuss emotions. Which of these groups of people do you find yourself naturally wanting to spend more time with? It's a no-brainer, right? Generally, we are more attracted to positivity than negativity.

Moral issues aside, being kind helps us in evolutionary terms too. If a person is easier to get along with, cooperative, caring and helpful, then they are more likely to be welcomed into a tribe to help secure its future than one who is trying to tear it down with their negative attitudes and actions. As with gratitude, kindness and love will go a long way in helping you move towards your dream work.

But there are other, arguably more important benefits as well. We are approaching the end of our journey, and have only this and one more lesson left. And as keen as we are to reach our destination, it is vital that we don't miss out on the important activity of sitting beneath the metaphorical *sakura* tree with our friends, families and loved ones to join together in the act of 'being'.

I promised I would stay away from clichés: I lied. Here it comes: *The past has gone, the future is not yet, all that is left is the present: and what a gift it is!* Joking aside, it is easy to miss the significance of this tired old maxim. To just 'be' is arguably the greatest goal we could ever attain.

When sitting around with those important to you, you may be tempted to glance at your watch and think about what you should be ticking off your 'to-do' list; to hold up a conversation while you check your social-media feed to see how well your latest 'boosted' advert is being received; to delay dinner, just for ten minutes, while you respond to that 'crucial' email. We've all done it. We've all ignored people in our 'nows' in favour of things in our 'tomorrows'.

Yet, even when you get to where you are going, as good as it will be, it will never replace the love that someone who truly loves you can offer. And why is that? Because, as the old saying goes, this is life's greatest gift to us all: to be loved and to love back in return.

I remember writing this in my journal:

Does God (universe or other),
Simply get tired of being alone,
And so creates 'other' than itself,
To love and to be loved in return?
Maybe that is what we are all about

While on the 88, as wonderful as it was that I could prove to myself that time and money need never stand in the way of our highest goals and ambitions, this wasn't the greatest takeaway.

It was the people I met along the way who helped me continue through the dark moments when I was battered and bruised physically, mentally and emotionally; the people who gave me the opportunity to develop my sense of compassion by offering me the chance to pass on the kindness that they had previously shown to me; the people who welcomed me into their homes for tea, a chat and a short respite from treading the roads. It was all these wonderful people who, in their own way, showed me love and also caused love to bud inside me. Looking back, this was the greatest takeaway.

Of course, with all this goodwill, gratitude and love flying around, you may discover that, on closer inspection, you are already in your ideal workplace. Maybe now, with a new improved attitude, you are finally receiving (or attracting) the recognition, professionally, socially and financially that you needed for this to be your 'dream work'. And that's okay. It's also okay, if it isn't.

Whether this chapter has confirmed that you need to move on, or, actually, there is nowhere else you need to be, matters not. What matters is that you never lose sight of the greatest goal behind *all* goals: to love and to allow another to love you back.

By all means build a magnificent future – I have given you plenty of encouragement to do so throughout this book – but don't do so at the expense of those who are with you, loving you, here, right now.

Take a moment to be grateful for all that they bring to your life, take another moment to love them back, and then, now lifted into a lighter mood, chase your dreams with gusto.

By the way, if you do want to test the theory that chanting a mantra can put you in a better mood, even if you have no clue what it's about, here is the phonetic version of the Japanese version I chanted on pilgrimage (and still chant to this day). Otherwise, skip it, and I'll see you over the page for our final chapter and lesson together.

Hannya Shingyo (The Heart Sutra)

Maka Hannya Haramita Shingyo
Kan ji zai bo za tsu
Gyo jin han ya ha ra mi ta
Ji sho ken go on kai ku
Do i sai ku
Yaku sha ri shi

Shiki fu i ku
Ku fu i shiki
Shiki soku ze ku
Ku soku ze shiki
Ju so gyo shiki

Yaku bu nyo ze
Sha ri shi
Ze sho ho ku so
Fu sho fu metsu
Fu ku fu jo
Fu zo fu gen
Ze ko ku chu

Mu shiki mu ju so gyo shiki
Mu gen ni bi ze shin i
Mu shiki sho ko mi soku ho
Mu gen kai nai shi mu i shiki kai
Mu mu myo yaku mu mu myo jin
Nai shi mu ro shi yaku mu ro shi jin
Mu ku shu metsu do mu chi yaku mu toku i

Mu sho toku ko bo dai sa ta e
Han ya ha ra mi ta ko
Shin mu ke ge mu ke ge ko
Mu u ku fu on ri i sai ten do mu so ku gyo ne

Han san ze sho butso e
Han ya ha ra mi ta ko
Toku a noku ta ra san myaku san bo dai
Ko chi han ya ha ra mi ta
Ze dai jin shu ze dai myo shu
Ze mu jo shu ze mu to do shu
No jo i sai ku shin jitsu fu ko
Ko setsu han ya ha ra mi ta shu
Soku setsu shu watsu

Gya tei gya tei
Ha ra gya tei
Hara so gya tei
Bo ji so wa ka
Hannya Shingyo

Lesson 9:
You have what it takes

'It is impossible to live without failing at something, unless you live so cautiously that you might as well not have lived at all – in which case, you fail by default.'

– J. K. Rowling

My journey ended where it had begun. I had completed, on foot, the 1,400km of the 88 Temple Pilgrimage and was returning to Ryozenji, Temple 1, to 'close the circle'. Although 88 temples constitute the entire pilgrimage, from a Buddhist perspective, for it to be considered complete you must retrace your steps back through all the temples from number 88 down, until, once again, you pass and bow through the gates of the first.

The feeling on completion was like nothing I'd ever experienced; a wonderful mix of euphoria and deep, peaceful stillness. I wrote this in my journal:

With an empty physical victory to hand,
The truth dawns
That the goal is not the win
But the nowness of creating it.

In Zen, the symbol of a circle (*ensō*) is significant, and it is represented in the pilgrimage by the route it takes around the circumference of the island of Shikoku. The *ensō* symbolises enlightenment, strength, elegance, the universe and, of course, never-ending cycles. This is an important element of Buddhism and equally important for those on the path of the Buddhist Millionaire.

The end is never the end

We have reached the final chapter of this book and the last lesson; almost at the end. But the end is never the end.

Just as waves roll upon a shore, then retreat slowly, and a breath draws in air from outside with an insistent pull, before releasing it gently, so will your life as a Buddhist Millionaire also ebb and flow.

Life, in all its expressions, will continue to circulate, endlessly peaking, troughing and peaking again through the arcs of the *ensō*. And herein lies the lesson of this chapter: that you have been here before, and that you most certainly have what it takes to succeed again.

The seven basic plots

In his book, *Why We Tell Stories*, Christopher Booker outlines the seven basic plots that authors use to tell their stories. There are, he suggests, only a certain number of ways in which a story can be told, and the differences come not in the plots, but in the way that they are expressed.* Just as in life.

One of the things that prevents many people from setting and chasing ambitious goals is self-doubt. They often wonder if they have what it takes to reach beyond the norm. If this is your experience, as it has been mine in the past, I'm here to tell you that you do indeed have what it takes to build the life of your choice, including one in which you enjoy meaningful, profitable work. But as always, true to the spirit of Buddhism, I don't expect you to take my word as gospel; instead, I advise that you delve into your past for evidence.

Although not always easy, life *is* simple. It just takes a while to get it right. There is no special information you need to know; no hidden secrets to master; no mystical success blueprints to study; you just need to stay in the game long enough to become accomplished. As with a fine whisky resting in barrels while its full flavour matures, there is nothing to add to the brew but time.

---

* The plots are: Overcoming the Monster, Rags to Riches, The Quest, Voyage and Return, Comedy, Tragedy and Rebirth.

The student becomes the master

I had taught Alice karate since she was seven years old, and now that she was sixteen, I thought, while lying on my back looking up at the ceiling, the time had come for her to attempt her Shōdan (black-belt exam).

For the first time ever, Alice had breached all of my defences and hit me square in the chest with the ball of her foot. I didn't see the kick coming – a surprise, given that speed and reaction are my fighting raison d'être. The force sent me sprawling across the polished wood floor, where I now lay, flat on my back, giggling. Alice, shy, studious, polite but brutal, ran over in panic. She had toppled her teacher. Alice was the first of my students to be awarded a black belt.

Just as there are only seven basic plots to any story, so can we guarantee that, one day, the student will surpass the master. Life is wonderfully predictable.

Humans like to believe they are completely autonomous. They are not. And this fact is a thorn-stemmed rose. We are more susceptible to others' thoughts, ideas, opinions and manipulations than we would care to admit. If you doubt this, from where do you think the foundational beliefs that guide the decisions of your life emerge? From your parents and environment, of course. Likewise, do you think that you are totally in control of your spending habits and buying decisions within the marketplace? You'd like to think so, right? The advertising and marketing industries would beg to differ.

Martin Lindstrom is a marketing visionary who has been on the front line of the branding industry for over twenty years. In his book, *Brandwashed*, he turns the spotlight on the industry, exposing the full extent of the psychological tricks and traps that companies devise to encourage us all to buy. It's an eye-watering read because it reveals how 'blind' we are to advertising and marketing tactics. But it is also an eye-opening read, for precisely the same reasons.

Once you've walked a path for any significant length of time, typically patterns begin to emerge. A business begins to identify 'typical buying behaviour'; an employee senses what is necessary to 'keep the boss happy'; an athlete understands that with enough practice, their performance statistics will rise. Walking a pilgrimage, which in itself is a microscopic representation of the macrocosm of life, similarly reveals life patterns. It could be said that anything and everything with a beginning, middle and end is a pilgrimage of sorts, with all the lessons and discoveries inherent in that process.

So, while the predictable endless round of a rising and setting sun may set off alarm bells in some, this predictability is really a reason to celebrate.

Success machines

You are a success machine. Even if you consider yourself

not very accomplished, the fact that you are reading this sentence proves that you *are* a success machine.

Your genes have survived an endless round of continuous improvement since the day they took those first tentative steps upon their Darwinian pilgrimage of evolution. Think about that little. This is no small matter. Even if, currently, you are living a life of terrible struggle that doesn't feel, in any shape or form, to be anything other than failure, you are still standing on the shoulders of many past successes.

Survival is a brutal, violent, painful process that favours only the strong. You – yes, you – with all your faults, frailties and follies, are one of life's survivors. Great job.

Interesting fact alert: the biological you that is you right now is not the same you as the you of before! Red blood cells live for about four months and are then replaced; white blood cells live longer, about a year, while skin cells only last two or three weeks and colon cells, just a few days. You are still 'you', of course, but regenerated, at least to some degree.

At the end of my pilgrimage, it dawned on me as I arrived at the Ryozenji temple that although I had been there before and, for all intents and purposes, was the same person, I could not have been more different, just like the body growing brand-new cells. This time I stood in the temple's grounds with the experience of hundreds and thousands of steps behind me. The place and I were the same, though worlds apart, because of the hardship I had endured and the insights I had gained along the way.

Allow me another example from the world of martial arts.

The fighting ballerinas of the Royal Ballet

Another seven: this time it represents the average number of years it takes a student in a top-quality martial-arts school to attain the coveted rank of black belt. The length of time implies that there is a great deal to learn to reach this iconic goal. There isn't. An average student practising a minimum of three times a week could, in all honestly, learn all the techniques within a year. Much of what is entailed in becoming an expert martial artist is repetition; practising the same old, same old, day in, day out.

In my mid-twenties, when I first started teaching martial arts in schools in and around London, I received a phone call from the Royal Ballet. They asked me to come and work with their younger students based at White Lodge, the live-in school situated in the heart of Richmond Park.

White Lodge exudes excellence. It's where some of the future stars are primed for a career in this most gruelling, yet beautiful, form of dance. Students between the ages of eleven and sixteen manage academic studies alongside the intense and unforgiving study of ballet. I myself have been involved in high-level martial arts under the tutelage of some intensely demanding instructors, and even

I gasped at some of the efforts these youngsters made to perfect their art.

Because of the dancers' propensity for hard work, discipline and focus, and the high level of coordination they achieve through their art, I was able to teach them every move that I had developed over fifteen years in just six weeks.

If you had placed me and these ballet students side by side and asked us all to demonstrate a set of martial-arts moves, an unknowing audience would not have been able to tell us apart. If, however, you asked us to fight to the death, there would be only one winner. Me.

Although these youngsters had learned the shell of the moves, the 'blacks and the whites', with relevant ease, it would take many years for them to learn the in-between stage, the 'grey zone', as I like to call it. It is the nuance and subtlety of these mid-zones that take years to master. While master and novice use the same techniques – after all, how many new ways can there be to kick and punch? – the expert is differentiated by the thousands of 'in-between' steps.

Success is a process, not an event

You are, literally, born to succeed.

Even if you only see the world in evolutionary terms, where the sole task of biology is to spread genes in order to continue life (and if this is your view, phew, I'm guessing you don't write poetry!), then you are still built for success. We can take this fact and use it to boost our confidence to secure our ideal work life. It doesn't matter where we choose to aim our powers of success creation – yesterday the survivor of harsh hunter-gatherer expeditions, today completing a gruelling marathon, tomorrow creating a life where you leap out of bed to do work that you love and which pays handsomely – success is success.

Success is a process, not an event. It is something bestowed upon the special few by the gods. No, success is much more beautifully and exotically mundane. It is a predictable process; much as Amazon has learned that if they 'suggest' enough products they think you 'might like' when you visit their website, then sure enough, one day, you will predictably hit the 'buy now' button. Amazon's algorithms are masters of walking the next step and keeping on until their task is done. And so too, should you.

The truth is – and both my agent and publisher might kick me for this – you don't need another book, or video tutorial, or anything else to tell you how to succeed. You are living, breathing proof that you already have the gifts, powers and strength necessary to do so. While you are enjoying this 'precious, human life', why not make the most of it?

What matters is that you have enough faith, respect and trust, if not in yourself, then at least in life, to crack on and mould your future precisely as you see fit.

Trust that the seeds of success lie within you, and your choices make them grow

One of the things I love most about being a writer is the freedom it provides: freedom of expression (depending on my editor's choice to let me take the reins) but also freedom of time.

While writing this book, I followed a strict routine: wake at 5am; get out of bed straight onto my meditation cushion for a 45-minute 'power-up session'; shower, then jump into the car to arrive at a 7am 'early risers' martial-arts class.

I return home around 9.15am, have coffee and then start writing. After spending the morning at the keyboard, I then do something I love just as much as writing: walking my Jack Russell dog, Smudge, in Richmond Park.

Walking Smudge is an utter delight. To watch a dog run free is joyful. Dogs live fully in the moment, seemingly with no distracting thoughts about yesterday's failures, fears of tomorrow or guilt for wholly enjoying this unique precious moment in the park among the deer.

The way dogs live echoes a key teaching in Buddhism that became clear to me while walking the 88, which is that much of the hardship in our lives is a result of our inability to fully accept and commit to the moment in which we find ourselves – unlike a dog! Instead we grasp and strain, always searching and reaching for something outside of the present moment.

Consider this teaching against the backdrop of your experience: at any given moment you are likely to be thinking either of a past that has already been and gone, or a future yet to arrive. Very rarely do you fully engage with the only time that actually exists: the present moment.

Why is this? Personally, I love to think ahead to what I could create and improve in the future. I love the buzz of creation and am often bored and stifled by the here and now, particularly if not much is going on, or worse, if what is going on is intolerable.

It is both the advantage and disadvantage of having a human brain: we can plan ahead with our advanced cognitive functions, but if we stay stuck in thought we fail to embrace and enjoy the moment. It is a tightrope that we have to walk carefully.

Although we must think ahead to plan our futures, it is important to recognise that the future is actually produced in the present. There can only ever be this moment, right here, right now. Just as the Buddhists say, the seeds of future success are inherent and released within the choices that we make in the present moment, just as they are in an acorn.

As summer draws to an end and the first signs of autumn appear, the oak trees in Richmond Park become laden with acorns. Squirrels busy themselves collecting and storing them, while deer feast on those that have dropped to the ground under the trees.

When you pick up an acorn and look at its tiny shell

topped with a latticed brown beret, it is difficult to believe that within it is the seed that will one day make a wonderful, gnarly, gargantuan oak tree; yet we know that it will happen. All around us are wonderful old oak trees born from acorns. The proof is right before our eyes.

So, in just the same way, you must trust that in choosing your path, the seeds of success are already inherent within your decision, and the efforts you put in will enable them to grow.

Patterns of success

As a final exercise, try this:

Take a sheet of paper and write down ten to twenty work-related successes that you have had to date. The successes can be either minor or major, or a mixture of the two, to reflect the realities of the workplace. For example, when I did this exercise I included washing my parents' car for pennies, landing my first Saturday job (in a camping shop in Kingston upon Thames), securing a teaching position at a top London tennis club, starting my own business and being offered a publishing contract. Any work-related 'win' is notable. (You can do this with subjects other than work, if you like – they will reveal your successes just as adequately.)

After a while, you may begin to notice that life, to some degree, has always taken care of your work and money needs. Even if you have hit rock bottom and needed handouts from friends, family or government, life has stepped in and helped. These low points in life are often overlooked. I believe that they are not indicators of failure, but on the contrary, evidence of life's inordinately creative ways of supplying just what you need, just when you need it. Countless biographies of well-known people cite either their bankruptcies and/or difficult backgrounds as reasons for their future success: Abraham Lincoln, Dave Ramsey, Walt Disney, P. T. Barnum, Cyndi Lauper, Elton John, J. K. Rowling and Oprah Winfrey, to name just some. Let's look at some of these in turn.

Abraham Lincoln: prior to his successful election as president of the United States of America in 1860, he successfully failed.

After his business partner died (they owned a general store in Salem, Illinois), Lincoln was left by himself to pay off mounting bank debts accrued to finance a shop inventory that didn't sell. Modern bankruptcy didn't exist in the 1830s and Lincoln was forced to spend the next seventeen years paying off his creditors.

Lincoln survived this turmoil, going on to become one of America's most notable heroes in his role as 'Saviour of the Union' and 'Emancipator of the Slaves'.

Dave Ramsey: Ramsey is arguably the most widely read and famous personal financial advisor in United States' history.

His popular radio programme (*The Dave Ramsey Show*) airs on 550 stations and reaches an estimated 8.5 million listeners, but Ramsey, like Lincoln, failed before he succeeded. Ramsey financed grand purchases for his previous real-estate business with credit and it proved to be his undoing. After creditors began to call in debts, he was left with no alternative but to file for bankruptcy.

His direct experience of money and business, both good and bad, gave him the insight that fuelled his reinvention as a relatable money 'guru'.

Walt Disney: the world-famous creator of cartoons started out life as a failure, in some people's eyes, filing for bankruptcy when still a teenager, and then again, a few years later.

Unperturbed, Disney, the serial entrepreneur, pursued another loan to finance yet another business. This time his family were the benefactors, and his company would go on to make the first full-length animated movie, *Snow White and the Seven Dwarfs*.

But even the company that would go on to help Disney amass an estimated $5 billion had its teething problems. The production costs of *Snow White* outstripped Disney's financial resources at the time and he faced yet another bankruptcy, as well as the possibility that the film might not be finished.

In one last desperate push, Disney took out another loan, the film was finished and the rest, as they say, is history. (*Snow White* grossed $6.5 million and became one of the most successful animated films ever made.)

P. T. Barnum: Barnum was the founder of the Barnum and Bailey Circus, the most famous circus of all time and the subject of the 2017 hit film *The Greatest Showman*. But prior to 1871 and his massive circus success, Barnum had endured a catalogue of hardships.

Motivated by crippling poverty in his youth, Barnum wanted to prove that he could be 'more'. At 25 he began his career as a showman. In 1841, he purchased Scudder's American Museum in New York City and financed the upgrade of both the run-down building and its exhibits. But after the building burned down (five times!) he was forced into bankruptcy.

Not to be beaten by adversity, Barnum made money lecturing about 'The Art of Getting Money', which paid his debts and set the stage for the beginning of his famous three-ring circus. He was 64 years old when he found his great success.

Cyndi Lauper: love it or loath it, Lauper's music success is indisputable, with her estimated net worth being around $30 million. But as with all our other celebrity examples, Lauper suffered hardship along the way.

Before her rise to fame, she sang and wrote for a band called Blue Angel. They released an album in 1980 – to virtually no public acclaim – and Lauper was forced to file for bankruptcy in 1981.

Bad times had previously struck. In 1977, doctors told her she would never sing again after severely damaging her vocal chords. However, six years later, in 1983, she released her hit album, *She's So Unusual*, which included hit classics such as: 'Girl's Just Want to Have Fun', 'Time After Time', 'All Through the Night', 'She Bop' and, fittingly, 'Money Changes Everything'.

Elton John: Elton John is one megastar you would never suspect had suffered the trials and tribulations that most ordinary folk have to endure along his path of glory.* But by now you'll have guessed that, yes, he did! Albeit in reverse.

John enjoyed success straight out of the gates with the release of his first single, 'Your Song', in 1970 (who doesn't love that song?). From there, he rose to super-stardom, with a number of albums, the most notable being *Goodbye Yellow Brick Road* and *Caribou*, released in 1973 and 1974 respectively.

But in 2002, the hardships that he had eluded so far in his career would come knocking. After blowing all his money on his infamous rock-and-roll lifestyle, everything came crashing down and he was forced to file for bankruptcy.

---

* Unless you watched the recent biopic of his life, *Rocketman*, which came out in cinemas in 2019.

In 2003, newly focused and ready to launch again, he signed a deal to perform 75 shows over three years at the iconic Caesar's Palace in Las Vegas. As of 2018, his estimated worth is $450 million. Maybe his next single could be called 'The Comeback Kid'.

J. K. Rowling: As a writer, I'm particularly fond of this celebrity example. Rowling has sold millions of copies of her books in 73 different languages, and she has accrued over $20 billion through film adaptations and sponsorship. But she too, unsurprisingly, has a backstory of hardship.

In the late 1990s, Rowling was contending with depression after the death of her mother, a failed marriage, a new baby daughter to raise alone, no job and sample chapters of a new book that was being rejected left, right and centre by publishers. She says that twelve publishers initially rejected her Harry Potter book proposal!

For Rowling, there was nowhere left to fall, she had hit the bottom but was still alive and so continued to do what she loved – writing.

'Failure meant a stripping-away of the essential. I stopped pretending to myself that I was anything other than what I was, and began to direct all my energy into finishing the only work that mattered to me,' says Rowling. It sounds remarkably like the lesson that Jim, my Japanese teacher's husband, taught me all those years ago.

Oprah Winfrey: 'I know for sure: Your journey begins with a choice to get up, step out, and live fully'. These are the words on the back cover of Oprah Winfrey's book, *What I Know for Sure*.

At 63 years old, Oprah Winfrey has amassed an impressive list of media accomplishments: she is the host and proprietor of the highest-rated US television show of all time (*The Oprah Winfrey Show*), she runs a television network (OWN), she has her own monthly glossy magazine (*O, The Oprah Magazine*); and is the richest African-American woman as well as the first and only black multi-billionaire in the US.

By contrast, her early life was a list of equally notable difficulties. Born in 1954 in Mississippi to a teenage single mother, she was so poor that she was sent to school wearing dresses made out of potato sacks. In 1986, she disclosed on her TV show that she was raped at the age of nine by a cousin, then again by other family members. She became pregnant at fourteen, but her son died prematurely. She has also talked repeatedly about her struggle with her weight and shame regarding her body image.

In spite of all these hardships, Oprah Winfrey is a woman who lives and breathes positivity: 'I think time is not put to best use focusing on where we haven't been,' she says. 'My thing is: do it. You want to see changes? Then get out there and make those changes yourself.'

I use these examples not because we need to aspire to

fame and glory (but equally, if you want to, why not?), but because the bright lights of celebrity often help to highlight a point: they all wanted something – they all struggled – they all got there in the end.

Remember that these people didn't start out famous. They are well known now not because they themselves are endowed with any hidden gift or power. They were once 'white belts', like us all. Their stories demonstrate the different ways in which life can spur us on to achieve our aspirations.

However, some people may argue that life's evolutionary priority is the simple goal of spreading genes rather than to facilitate our success in the modern world. Initially, it may be true that survival was life's highest ambition; but life progresses. In days gone by, according to Maslow's Hierarchy of Needs diagram (see chapter 2), life was just about obtaining the essential needs for survival such as air, water, sex, somewhere to sleep and the like. Later, as we progressed, it included more subtle needs such as self-esteem, confidence, achievement and both respect for, and by, others.

The fact is that we are designed to evolve and exhibit our highest capacities, and life has a vested interest in helping us to do so.

So, take comfort in this knowledge and the other eight lessons that precede it, and get out there and make a spectacular life for yourself. Set your bar high. Why would you *not* expect to live a life where work, an occupation to which you devote a third of your life, is inspiring, meaningful *and* rewarding?

Dare to ask big things of yourself, because in the end, in the spirit of the endless cycle of the *ensō*, it will be your turn, as the new master, to pass on this help to your students, who will be eagerly looking to you for instruction.

And the turn of circle will have begun all over again.

Conclusion:
Indra's net

In the Huayan school of Chinese Buddhism, the story of 'Indra's net' is used to describe the interconnectedness of the universe.

The story goes that the great god Indra owns a net that stretches out to infinity. In each eye of the net hangs a glittering jewel – all the jewels glittering like the stars in an endless sky. In the polished surface of any single jewel it is possible to see reflected all the others, infinite in number, and all the others reflect the single jewel in return.

Similar to Indra's net, the nine lessons of this book all reflect, and live in, one another. Lesson 9, for instance, trusting that you have what it takes to achieve your goals naturally reflects Lesson 1, where you choose what it is you want in the first instance. Faith in yourself leads to the successful attainment of chosen goals and in turn builds more faith and freedom to choose further, ad infinitum.

I have spoken about the lessons I learned while on the

88 Temple Pilgrimage in the context of creating work that is both meaningful (and enjoyable) as well as profitable, but they can be used for any goal. I have chosen to deal with the subject of work because, on my return from Japan, I noticed that it was the cause of most people's hardship, at least among those who I was spending time with.

A holy man I met on the pilgrimage had told me that it was my duty to share what I had learned for the betterment of the world and its people. Initially, I did this by recounting my experiences in my book, *The Hardest Path*. Later it became clear that the lessons could be used more pointedly to deal with money, a subject that affects every one of us, no matter our gender, race, colour or creed, and one that drives so many of our work, life and business decisions.

Much of a pilgrimage is walked in total silence; the idea is to allow the answers that you seek to bubble up unobscured by frivolous chatter. The wisdom bestowed upon a pilgrim can then be 'heard' more clearly and pondered upon and then translated into whatever format necessary to help and serve others.

It took some years for me to realise that these great insights from one of the world's great spiritual trails could be used for a subject as mundane as money. There came a time, however, when I realised that the subject of money cannot be avoided, even from within the pious tower in which I suspect I had been hiding.

The turning point came when I was watching His Holiness the Dalai Lama on YouTube. He was delivering a talk on compassion to a congregation of thousands of wide-eyed followers, all bathing in his spiritual presence. For some reason, I homed in on his robes.

As simple and unpretentious as his maroon and saffron threads were I couldn't escape the thought that some-where along the line money would have had to have been spent to keep this great spiritual icon clothed. In that moment, the inextricable link between a life of meaning and finances came sharply into focus and I decided that a conversation about money must ensue.

This book, then, is that conversation. They are lessons of life that I came to understand finally and clearly while on pilgrimage, free from the obscuration of day-to-day living. You don't need to walk a pilgrimage to discover them; I just happened to discover them while doing so.

As a reminder, these are:

1. **Start from where you are**

   Of course, it's impossible to be anywhere other than where you are right now. Whether you are satisfied with your starting position or not does nothing to change fact. Acknowledge it. Accept it. Move forward from it, but never deny it. For now, you are where you are, and who you are, and it's as good a place as any to begin to decide what you want, and where you want to go.

2. **The art of 'one-stepping'**

   From where you begin, there is only one direction of travel: forward. Life, or indeed any journey, can sometimes feel overwhelming, and uncertainty can often lead to procrastination and inaction. When this happens, simply focus on one small immediate task, the next single step on your adventure. There is no need to concern yourself with the many steps you must take miles from here; you can deal with them once you arrive there. And when you do, they will simply be another immediate single step for you to tread.

3. **When the student is ready, the teacher appears**

   Sometimes you won't know what your next step should be. In this instance, buoyed by your commitment to action once you know what this is to be, rest assured that the teacher of your next move will appear. It may come within the sentence of a book, from an insight while out on a walk, a comment from a friend or, quite literally, a teacher with the answers that you seek. Keep your eyes, ears and mind open to the wisdom that will inform.

4. **The art of effortlessness**

   To tell you to try not to try too hard is a contradiction in terms, but however challenging this may be, it is worth the effort! Relax a little. Let go of the reins. It's not essential for you to have everything figured out to succeed. Remember that the sun came up long before you were born, and it will set long after you are gone. Why not just enjoy its colours and warmth while you are here, without interfering?

5. **The art of meditation**

This is arguably the single most important skill that any sentient being can develop. It is vital on so many levels. Among other things, it will help you tap into latent inner resources, develop laser focus for tackling important tasks, reduce stress in difficult times and provide a way of looking at your life, work included, that will either help you reach where you want to go or, equally, find value in the spot on which you currently stand.

6. **The law of karma**

Things will go wrong. To deny this is not only to do yourself a disservice but also to misunderstand the vicissitudes of life. With a fresh perspective, problems can be used not only as fuel for future success, but also to provide insight into ourselves.

7. **Invisible currencies**

Not everything of value is measurable in money. In fact – and it has been argued in song many times – 'The Best Things in Life are Free'. When your measure of success is solely fiscal, you are setting yourself up for a mighty fall. Wearing 'money only' specs, you fail to see the 'invisible currencies' – those things that have great value but cannot be immediately exchanged for pounds and pence – and you may be tempted prematurely to abort your ambitious plans when they were just about to bloom.

8. **Love, gratitude and the heart (sutra)**

It's an old cliché to say 'love the journey not just the destination', but as hackneyed as it is, there is no better way to make this point. As you travel the journey (another cliché for which I am not at all sorry) towards your ideal work life, remember to show love and appreciation along the way. Be grateful for where you've been, where you currently stand and for what is to come; take time to listen and chat with the people you meet; love the wins, the losses, the process and, above all, yourself, and the work that you will be giving to the world.

9. **You have what it takes**

You have a track record of success, a history littered with 'small wins': learning to walk, your first kiss, passing your driving test, at last keeping your temper in check, recovering from a health scare, having children, not having children – the list is endless. Take note of the proclivity you have to 'get the job done'. Life is on your side, no matter the goal. Pick what you want, and do yourself a favour; go and get it. After all, why break the habit of a lifetime?

Ultimately, it doesn't matter how you get there, what

matters that is you get going. I urge you not to wait.

Life is a work in progress and so too are the findings of science, religion and philosophy. I have drawn upon factual information from all three disciplines and hope that you have found this both interesting and beneficial, but, in the spirit of Buddhism, I have mainly written from direct experience, and from the experiences of the other Buddhist Millionaires I interviewed. It is up to you to add to and update this reservoir of knowledge by creating your own experiences, discovering your own truths and carving your own unique model of life.

If it is still not yet clear, then let me reiterate here: to be a Buddhist Millionaire, it is not necessary to be either a Buddhist or a millionaire. The term is applicable to anyone who is committed to meaningful work in which they are engrossed and about which they are passionate (as you might expect in a Buddhist), and making good money in the process (as you might expect of a millionaire). I'll leave it up to you to decide which of our interviewees are Buddhist Millionaires in the literal as well as the metaphorical sense of the term.

I sincerely hope that this book serves you well and maybe, one day, I might wake up to an email or Facebook message where you let me know that the actions that it precipitated changed your work life irrevocably.

In your message, you might say that you have never loved work as much as you do right now, and that financially you are in the best place you have ever been. You might tell me that you overcame some early setbacks, but carried on with your work vision regardless. And, guess what, you might say: you were right, it did all work out just fine in the end!

But the best part of the message will be that, buoyed by your success, you have now started to help others do the same, as they turn to you for advice on living a life enriched with profitable, enjoyable and meaningful work. And this will be the moment when I call out from my laptop to my wife:

'Hey, Shez, check out this lovely message I just received from a reader. I think we've got ourselves a new Buddhist Millionaire.'

Gratitudes

Does anyone other than those being thanked read the acknowledgements (I prefer the term 'gratitudes') part of a book? They should, and I wish I had earlier in my career. At a certain stage in life, we understand that success cannot be achieved, or enjoyed, without a team. None of us, as they say, are islands.

Many wonderful people are involved in the book that you hold in your hand, today. I hope that public acknowledgement of their efforts in some way lets them know how much I appreciate what they have done for this project. So here goes. Thank you to: Michael Taylor, Selina Lamy, Drew Sullivan, Charles Negromonte, Sunni Jardine, Cheree Strydom, Ian McClelland, Druhv Baker, George Asprey, Gary Chamberlain, Moatez Jomni and Matt Hastings for sharing your inspiring stories; the wonderful team at Short Books, particularly the fabulous Helena Sutcliffe who has given her heart and soul to this book and improved it with her input (she could do with bending her knees a little more when playing tennis though!); to my Sheri, who quite simply needs an award for putting up with me (all partners of writers will understand the challenge); the inimitable Frances Cutts who has and will always be my first port of call when seeking advice – it's always good to know you're in my corner; and to Renata Kasprzak, my agent, who backed me from the very beginning and helped me cross the bridge from idea to reality – here's to many more.

The last and maybe most important thanks goes to you, the reader who has taken the time and effort, not to mention paid the money, and invested in the ideas and pages of this book. Thank you. I hope they serve you well and that you end up enjoying doing work that you adore.

Endnotes

1 'Divorces in England and Wales', 2016. Office for National Statistics. https://www.ons.gov.uk/peoplepopulation andcommunity/birthsdeathsandmarriages/divorce/bulletins/ divorcesinenglandandwales/2016

2 'Recession linked to over 10,000 suicides across Europe, North America'. *British Journal of Psychiatry,* 2014. https:// www.sciencedaily.com/releases/2014/06/140612085801.htm

3 Hempstead KA, Phillips JA, 2015. 'Rising suicide among adults aged 40–64 years: The role of job and financial circumstances'. *American Journal of Preventative Medicine* 48(5):491–500.

4 Yuval Noah Harari, 2014. *Sapiens: A Brief History of Humankind.*

5 Michael Taylor, *Bankers Anonymous*. https://www.bankers-anonymous.com/about/

6 'How the PPI Scandal Unfolded', 2011. *The Guardian.* https://www.theguardian.com/business/2011/may/05/ how-ppi-scandal-unfolded

7 Hans Kruuk, 1972. *Surplus Killing by Carnivores.*

8 *The American Heritage Dictionary of the English Language*, Fifth Edition, 2020. Houghton Mifflin Harcourt Publishing Company.

9 Hannah Jane Parkinson. 2018. 'Would you take £1m now, or £1,000 a week for the rest of your life?' *The Guardian.* https:// www.theguardian.com/commentisfree/2018/mar/29/would-you-take-1m-now-or-1000-a-week-for-the-rest-of-your-life

10 'How Many People Volunteer and What Do They Do?', 2019. *UK Civil Society Almenac.* https://data.ncvo.org.uk/volunteering

Matt Jardine is a martial artist, entrepreneur, public speaker, podcaster, teacher, and the founder of Jardine Karate School. His previous books include *Mo and Lucy – Choices*, and *The Hardest Path*, inspired by his 88 Temple Pilgrimage of Japan. Matt has practised meditation and other Eastern arts for over 25 years and now lives in London with his wife and Jack Russell.